Yankee Stadium

Yankee Stadium

Drama, Glamor, and Glory

BY RAY ROBINSON
AND CHRISTOPHER JENNISON

VIKING STUDIO

FRONTISPIECE: JULY 4, 1961, AND THE BIG BALL PARK IS JAMMED.
TITLE PAGE: A WIDE-ANGLE VIEW OF YANKEE STADIUM, TAKEN IN
1996. ATTENDANCE WOULD IMPROVE AS THE YANKEES FLEXED
THEIR PENNANT MUSCLES.

VIKING STUDIO
Published by the Penguin Group
Penguin Group (USA) Inc., 375 Hudson Street, New York, New York 10014, U.S.A.
Penguin Books Ltd, 80 Strand, London WC2R 0RL, England
Penguin Books Australia Ltd, 250 Camberwell Road, Camberwell, Victoria 3124, Australia
Penguin Books Canada Ltd, 10 Alcorn Avenue, Toronto, Ontario, Canada M4V 3B2
Penguin Books India (P) Ltd, 11 Community Centre, Panchsheel Park, New Delhi–110 017, India
Penguin Books (N.Z.) Ltd, Cnr Rosedale and Airborne Roads, Albany, Auckland, New Zealand
Penguin Books (South Africa) (Pty) Ltd, 24 Sturdee Avenue, Rosebank, Johannesburg 2196, South Africa

Penguin Books Ltd, Registered Offices:
80 Strand, London WC2R 0RL, England

First Published in 1998 by Viking Studio,
a member of Penguin Group (USA) Inc.

10   9   8   7   6   5   4   3   2   1

Grateful acknowledgment is made for permission to reprint an excerpt from "Baseball and Writing"
from *The Complete Poems of Marianne Moore*.
Copyright © Marianne Moore, 1961. Copyright renewed Lawrence E. Brinn and Louise Crane,
Executors of the Estate of Marianne Moore, 1989. By permission of Viking Penguin, a division of
Penguin Books USA Inc.

Illustration credits appear on page 182.

CIP data available

ISBN 0-670-87093-5
ISBN 0-670-03301-4
Printed in the United States of America
Text font set in Janson, display font set in Blackoak

DESIGNED BY RENATO STANISIC

To Nancy and Lee, for whom Yankee
Stadium has always been a home away from home.
R.R.

In loving memory of my father, Keith, who took me to Yankee
Stadium the first time, and many times.
C.J.

. . . .

Studded with stars in belt and crown,
the Stadium is an adastrium.
O flashing Orion,
your stars are muscled like the lion.

Marianne Moore,
poet, 1956

Yankee Stadium

American League Park, New York.

ABOVE: Long before there was a Yankee Stadium or Yankees, for that matter, the New York Highlanders played at Hilltop Park, located in the Washington Heights section of Manhattan. They played there from 1903 through the 1912 season, at which point they moved into the Polo Grounds and became tenants of the lordly New York Giants. Hilltop Park was demolished in 1914. The Columbia-Presbyterian Medical Center now occupies the site. BELOW: A view of Hilltop Park's left-field line and grandstand. For this game against the Washington Senators, the grandstand has been filled, and spectators are crowded around the edge of the field.

FIRST THERE WAS HILLTOP PARK, WITH A TEAM CALLED THE HIGHLANDERS, WHICH SOUNDED MORE BRITISH THAN AMERICAN. HILLTOP OPENED IN 1903, DURING THE PRESIDENCY OF THE CELEBRATED ROUGH RIDER, TEDDY ROOSEVELT. THAT SAME YEAR THE WRIGHT BROTHERS CHALLENGED THE HEAVENS WITH THEIR POWERED AIRPLANE, AND HENRY FORD'S AUTO BECAME AN IDEA WHOSE TIME HAD COME.

THE HIGHLANDERS WERE LOCATED IN UPPER MANHATTAN, THE BOROUGH THAT ALREADY HOUSED THE NATIONAL LEAGUE'S NEW YORK GIANTS. UNDER THEIR COMBATIVE LEADER, John J. McGraw, the Giants had responded heroically at the Polo Grounds to their manager's angry commands. On the west bank of the Harlem River, nestled beneath Coogan's Bluff, the Giants dominated the baseball world. They were gutty, snappy, and talented. Certainly no upstart team named the Highlanders, representing the newly formed American League, could threaten the Giants' supremacy in the raucous environs of New York. McGraw snarled that the Highlanders should be called the Invaders.

Hilltop Park was built in six hectic weeks, possibly a record in the baseball construction business. After Frank Farrell and Big Bill Devery plunked down $18,000 to buy the Baltimore Orioles franchise, they said they intended to transfer the club to New York—which is exactly what they did. Boasting dubious ethical credentials, these two operators underlined the brand of wheeler-dealer tactics it took in those brawling times to gain a niche in the burgeoning market of professional baseball.

Farrell was an ex-bartender and saloon proprietor, who placed bets on his own stable of racehorses. Devery also had varied talents: bartender, prizefighter, and policeman. In the last role he graduated to chief of police, although in some quarters he was known to be more corrupt than most of the criminals he pursued. In those days, however, there was no fingerpointing authority to judge a person's character or business ethics. Though Farrell and Devery were hardly eligible for the Social Register, their efforts to bring a club into New York as part of the nascent American League were applauded by Byron Bancroft "Ban" Johnson, an enterprising former sportswriter. Johnson had become the driving force behind the new league and was determined to challenge McGraw, at a time when the Giants had a stranglehold on the city's baseball patronage.

The Highlanders' two new owners appointed coal merchant Joseph Gordon as their president and hired the White Sox's Clark Griffith as manager. Griffith was widely acclaimed as the "Old Fox" and in later years changed his venue to Washington, where he owned the Washington Senators. He was also expected to pitch every now and then for the Highlanders.

Faced with a deadline of three months to find a suitable site for the Highlanders, Farrell and Devery selected and leased a plot in the Washington Heights section of Manhattan, between 165th and 168th Streets, on the west side of Broadway. The land was two blocks east of the Hudson River, and some insisted that the site was the most elevated location in the borough. It had been owned by the New York Institute for the Blind, but unfortunately the residents of the institute couldn't appreciate the magnificent view offered of the river and the majestic New Jersey Palisades.

Work got under way immediately to convert the site into a baseball park. Some $200,000 was spent to excavate the area, which was filled with debris and rocks. At the Broadway edge of the field, there was a marsh that had to be filled in with thousands of cubic yards of earth. When the construction was completed,

From the plain of the Harlem River it looms up like the great pyramid of Cheops from the sands of Egypt.

F. C. Lane,
April 1923 issue of
Baseball magazine

at a cost of $75,000, the park had 16,000 seats but was still quite swampy in spots and had an outfield that sloped unevenly. In a few years, a roof was installed over the single-decked wooden grandstand. The rickety fence, twenty feet high, that surrounded the outfield was festooned with advertising signs, which was the custom of most ball parks in that era—and hasn't changed much since.

"The ball park was the quintessence of urban leisure, watching others do things," Gunther Barth has written. "The scene seemed timeless to the spectators. Engulfed by the surging city, an urban tide flooding the land with a sea of houses, the baseball field exposed within its boundaries the remnants of a ravaged countryside in the form of scarred ravines protected by their ugliness from building construction."

Fans who attended games at Hilltop, also known as American League Park, couldn't see the churning waters of the Hudson or the Palisades unless they turned around to face them. Home plate faced Broadway, and as spectators sat on the wooden benches under their straw hats and bowlers, they yelled at almost every play. Standing was permitted on parts of the field. Sometimes people stood in the outfield and between the foul lines, thus often making it difficult for umpires to perform their role properly. It was also not unusual for players to be jostled and interfered with, depending on the loyalties of the fans. A common ritual at Hilltop was the passing around of a hat, so that fans could reward their heroes, few of whom were growing rich for their efforts.

Despite the efforts of the Giants' owner, John T. Brush, to derail the construction of Hilltop (he even tried to persuade the city fathers to have a street cut through the property), the ball park opened for business on a bright April 30 in 1903. The parade to the flagpole was led by none other than Ban Johnson himself, as the 69th Regiment Band played "Yankee Doodle" and "Columbia, the Gem of the Ocean." Farrell and Devery, in a box behind the Highlanders' bench, invited many of their political cronies, including Tammany's Big Tim and Little Tim Sullivan, to join them at the festivities.

To add to the patriotic motif of the occasion, every person who entered Hilltop was given a tiny American flag. The Highlander players were appropriately decked out in new white uniforms and white flannel caps with black lacing. The 16,000 fans (there may have been more, for there were plenty of standees) got their money's worth, as the new team in town defeated the Washington Senators, 6–2, behind their good-humored spitballer, Jack Chesbro. Wee Willie Keeler, the right-fielder, who may actually have said "Hit 'em where they ain't," that most durable of baseball maxims, starred in the opener, hitting two doubles and scoring three runs. Wee Willie, presumed to be on the downgrade, was one of the few shining lights on the Highlanders' roster. Big Ed Delahanty, who hit four home runs in a game in 1896, was the top name on the Washington club.

To everyone's surprise, the Highlanders managed to finish fourth in 1903. So expectations were high in 1904 that Griffith's club might even do better. They did. The hardworking Chesbro won a total of 41 games, still a major-league record. But what he is mainly remembered for—much as Bill Buckner is remembered for one ball that slithered under his first-baseman's glove in the 1986 World Series—is a wild throw that lost the pennant for the Highlanders. On the final day of the season, the Highlanders were one game back of the Boston Red Sox (also known at the time as the Pilgrims), with a doubleheader on tap between the two teams at Hilltop.

Needing a sweep to win the American League flag, the Highlanders came into the ninth inning of the first game tied with Boston at 2–2. With a man on third for the Red Sox, Chesbro unleashed a toss to his shortstop that rolled away far enough to permit the winning run to come trotting home. That the Highlanders came back to take the second game, behind southpaw Ambrose Putnam, was of no consequence. The fans, who had jammed Hilltop, went home disappointed.

That set the stage for years of frustration and failure at Hilltop, even though they corralled a star or two for their cast. In 1905, along came the notorious Prince Hal Chase, from California, a marvelously adept defensive first-baseman. Chase had enough charm and brains to lure the birds out of the magnolias. He too often walked a crooked mile, however. He was a cocky knave of diamonds with a habit of betting on ball games, more often than not against his own team. He was the only thing worth watching at Hilltop—but he had to be watched off the field, too. (Ultimately, Chase would be linked with the conspiracy to fix the 1919 Black Sox World Series.) Despite his suspicious behavior, Chase stayed with the Highlanders until 1913.

Several years after Hilltop's heralded beginnings, the team was doing poorly on the field and at the gate. Things were in such dismal shape that one New York baseball writer remarked that "if attendance falls any lower they'll have to put fractions on the turnstiles." At the same time, the haughty Giants were playing winning ball and drawing crowds of 30,000 at the Polo Grounds, including an impressive share of Broadway's most celebrated theatrical artists and jaunty politicos.

The Highlanders also managed to put the Senators' Walter Johnson on the first step to pitching immortality. In 1908, within the space of four days, Johnson pitched three shutouts at Hilltop Park against the hapless Highlanders. In the three

shutouts, Johnson—a raw-boned, quiet fellow out of Idaho—permitted a total of only twelve hits, while striking out twelve. Had it not been for the blue laws that prohibited the playing of professional baseball on Sundays, Johnson might have had his fourth shutout in less than a week. Chesbro was so disgusted with the performance of his own team that he hit the unsuspecting Johnson on the arm with an errant pitch.

By midseason of 1908, Farrell and Devery, constantly examining the financial bottom line, were also trying to run things on the field. This provoked Clark Griffith into walking out of his manager's post. In need of a pilot, the two men called on the Highlander shortstop, Norman "Kid" Elberfeld, to take over the reins. A hardheaded personality, every bit as tough on his own players as he was on opponents and umpires, Elberfeld presided over a winning percentage scarcely higher than his own modest batting average. By the season's end, Elberfeld was gone.

In 1909 and 1910 George Stallings, a former Georgia plantation owner, was installed as the resident genius. He finished second in 1910, bringing some excitement to Hilltop. The sourness between the Highlanders and the Giants even disappeared long enough for the two teams to engage in the first postseason City Series in New York history. Of course, the Highlanders had little to lose, while the Giants could no longer afford to ignore their upstart rivals from Washington Heights. The games alternated between Hilltop Park and the Polo Grounds, with the Giants of Christy Mathewson, Fred Merkle, Rube Marquard, Larry Doyle, and company emerging on top, as expected.

McGraw was satisfied that his Giants had made it clear that the Highlanders didn't belong on the same planet with his club. What's more, he felt that the Highlanders didn't belong in the same borough. Many fans must have felt the same way, too, for the Highlanders' attendance continued to drag.

It took a suspicious fire in the Polo Grounds in April 1911, which destroyed most of the wooden stands (a few days after the season's opener), to produce something of a rapprochement between the clubs. No adequate explanation was ever offered for the disaster, but there was no shortage of paranoid rumors circulating around New York. One popular yarn insisted that a platoon of hated Chicago Cubs fans had put a match to the vendor's stand. Another story hinted darkly that the Cubs' manager, Frank Chance, a bitter enemy of McGraw's, had actually lit the match himself. Those with a more inventive bent charged it was a Bolshevik plot. McGraw was perfectly willing to settle for Ban Johnson as the culprit, however.

Since the Giants had to keep playing their games, they were forced to crawl, cap in hand, to the knee of the much-despised Farrell. They asked him for a temporary tenancy at Hilltop Park. If the situation had been reversed, it is inconceivable that McGraw would have given Farrell's Highlanders the right time—or even two complimentary tickets. But acting as the consummate gentleman, Farrell granted the homeless Giants' request. Grateful for Farrell's unexpected civility, John Brush expressed himself in the manner of the day: "That Farrell is a real white man to come to our aid like that." So until late June, by which time the damage to the Polo Grounds had been repaired, the Giants played their home games at Hilltop.

The American League games continued to go on at Hilltop as usual. But it fell to Ty Cobb of the Detroit Tigers to provide the excitement. As he had so many times before in other ball parks, Cobb put his tempestuous stamp on Hilltop. In 1912, with the Tigers visiting the Highlanders, Cobb roared into the stands one afternoon and brutally assaulted a fan who had been baiting him. It turned out that the hapless victim had no hands.

The next day Ban Johnson suspended Cobb indefinitely, even though it wasn't clear whether Cobb had been aware of his target's physical condition. When the Detroit players went on strike, protesting the suspension, Cobb asked his teammates, most of whom detested him, to call it off. The strike ended in a day, as Cobb wound up with a $50 fine and a ten-day suspension.

The Giants' presence on the Highlanders' diamond failed to rub any magic off on the home team. The Highlanders continued to lose and continued to change managers, much in the manner of French cabinet switches. Hal Chase was tried for a while. With all of his guile, he failed. Minor-league manager Harry Wolverton was hired but for little more than a cup of coffee. Even the old Cubs hero, Frank Chance, assumed the managerial role in 1913. But he threw one too many temper tantrums with Farrell and left before the year was over. Chance was followed by shortstop Roger Peckinpaugh, who brought the club home in sixth place.

Farrell and Devery fought with each manager and with each other. It was obvious that if an American League franchise was to succeed in New York that new money and new front-office management had to be put in place. When the Highlanders' lease expired at Hilltop after the 1912 season, the Giants decided to repay Farrell's earlier hospitality. They allowed the lowly Highlanders to become co-tenants at the Polo Grounds, a state of affairs that would have been unthinkable a few years before.

For some time, the very name of the Highlanders had been a source of minor irritation in New York's newspaper offices. The nickname simply couldn't be squeezed comfortably into headline space. An innovative fellow named Jim Price, the sports editor of *The New York Press*, began calling the team the Yankees, preferring the breezy seven letters to the Highlanders' cumbersome eleven. The alteration stuck. The Yankees is what they have been known as ever since, perhaps the most celebrated nickname in the history of American team sports.

Whether they were dubbed the Yankees or High-landers, though, the team was bleeding, and Farrell and Devery knew it. They were aching to sell out, the sooner the better. The Giants, of course, were not for sale, though supplicants often approached McGraw on the subject. One day, after two such individuals were turned away by McGraw, he suggested that they speak to the Highlanders' owners.

One of the men was Colonel Jacob Ruppert, who had been fortunate enough to inherit a profitable brewery from his immigrant father. Ruppert's colonelcy was strictly honorary, having been bestowed on him by New York's governor, David Hill, in 1889. There was as little reason for the appointment as there was for the designation of Kentucky colonels, but Ruppert carried the title proudly.

Despite having been born on Manhattan's Upper East Side in 1867, Ruppert was never able to shake off his thick German accent, so appropriate for the York-ville area in which the Ruppert Brewery nestled. Ruppert had originally intended going to Columbia's School of Mines, but the lure of his father's business was stronger.

With substantial support from Tammany Hall, Ruppert got himself elected to Congress four times. As a wealthy, debonair young man about Manhattan, who had a valet to lay out his clothes for him each morning, Ruppert was rarely without a derby, causing sports columnist W. O. McGeehan to label him "The Man in the Iron Hat." The colonel was also interested in col-lecting things like racehorses, yachts, prize St. Bernard dogs, first editions, and monkeys. So it was only natural for him to attempt to add one of the town's ball clubs to his mound of possessions.

Although no fervent baseball fan, Ruppert occa-sionally attended games at the Polo Grounds with John McGraw. After he made a bid of $150,000 for the Giants, Ruppert turned down a chance to buy the Chicago Cubs. "I don't want any part of them," he

As a youngster, I never got over the experience of walking up the ramps toward my grandstand seat at Yankee Stadium and see-ing the slivers of green grass teas-ing me until it finally unfolded in full upon reaching my section. God! You could comfortably have put a dozen homes out there! And to think that three men cover all that territory. When I went to work some years later for the Yan-kees, I got chills when I discov-ered the old clubhouse safe-the only thing that actually went back to 1903. On each drawer of the Mosler safe were the stenciled names of original Highlanders-Chesbro, Keeler, Griffith, Fultz, etc. The chances are that not a single modern Yankee knew they were stuffing their wallets right where these old-timers had.

Marty Appel,
former publicity director
of the Yankees

said, agreeing with writer Edmund Wilson, who casti-gated Chicago as "a metallic junk heap of a modern American city." Just when Ruppert appeared to lose interest in baseball, McGraw introduced him to Cap-tain Tillinghast L'Hommedieu Huston, whose longi-tudinal name might have been bestowed as a joke. But Captain Huston was no joke. Born in Cincinnati to a family of modest means, he had gone to Cuba at the outset of the Spanish-American War as an engineer-ing officer. When hostilities ended, he stayed on to exercise his talents as an engineer, working mainly on harbor improvements. Within a few years he had be-come a millionaire and was hardly reluctant to tell people about it.

Urged on by the irrepressible Ban Johnson, who was still eager to place an American League franchise into a strong competitive position vis-à-vis the Giants, Ruppert and Huston approached Farrell and Devery.

They were aware that they held a distinct bargaining advantage, since they had carefully examined the books of the Highlanders/Yankees and found that the club was overburdened with debts and other obligations. Despite the debts, Ruppert and Huston were excited about the prospect of owning the Yankees. The two men may have had marked personality differences, but they shared the kind of tough ambition that so personified the city of New York. Probably they had never heard of Philip Hone, who had been mayor of New York City in 1826 and 1827. But they would have agreed with one of Hone's remarks, written in his diary: "The spirit of pulling down and building up is abroad. The whole of New York is rebuilt about once in ten years," wrote Hone, who had made a fortune in the auction business.

Now, some ninety years later, this was more true than ever about the kinetic city. Full of near-manic drive and fueled by the inexhaustible input of its swelling, hardworking immigrant population, the city benefited from men like Ruppert and Huston, who had the ego, willingness, and money to fulfill their vision. As the 1920s approached, New York had emerged as a pulsating, ever-changing entertainment bazaar, with its bustling Broadway, its gaudy and glittering Times Square, its Carnegie Hall, its Polo Grounds, its Madison Square Garden, its fashionable Fifth and Park Avenues, its Wall Street. By now it was incontestably America's cultural and economic capital. In the words of writer W. L. George, it was "all cities rolled into one, the only American city where people work and play, in others they work."

Ruppert and Huston weren't sociologists or historians but they sensed that baseball, like nearly everything else in New York, was ready to explode without any boundaries. The tough-talking, hard-drinking Huston enjoyed the company of ballplayers and journalists. He was much more gregarious than Ruppert, who was seemingly aloof from everything except money. But the colonel was a person who liked to win in life and games—his dogs and horses were invariably

prizewinners—and it was that quality that was originally so attractive to Huston.

Negotiations between Ruppert-Huston and Farrell-Devery were mercifully brief. The talking stage, which began late in 1914, ended not long after, with a bid of $460,000. By the morning of January 11, 1915, Ruppert and Huston had become fifty-fifty owners of the Yankees. Ban Johnson, relieved that the franchise hadn't passed into the hands of someone he didn't know or like, was delighted with the turn of events. So was the New York press, which was tired of covering the internecine squabbles between Farrell and Devery. What Johnson and the press couldn't fully appreciate at the time was that the deal represented a watershed moment, not only for New York's sports environment but for the structure and history of major-league baseball as well.

It wasn't long before Farrell and Devery disappeared into the woodwork. Devery died in 1919, almost penniless. When Farrell died, in 1926, his estate was judged to be less than $1,500.

Now the two new owners set about to infuse energy and purpose into their Yankees. Still sharing the Polo Grounds with their tyrannical landlord, McGraw, there was nothing as yet they could do about a new ball park. What they could do was hire a new manager, which became their first order of business.

They came up with Wild Bill Donovan, who had been a first-rate pitcher for Detroit, as well as a successful minor-league manager for the Providence club of the International League. The Yankees needed much more than Bill Donovan, however. Their crying need was for new talent on the field. In this area, they got some help from owner Frank Navin of Detroit, who was as eager as Ban Johnson for New York to produce a viable American League team. Navin permitted a young first-baseman named Wally Pipp and outfielder Hugie High to go to the Yankees on waivers. Pipp was hardly enough to turn a chronic loser around, but he ultimately was to play a dramatic, if unwitting role in Yankee history.

In 1916 and 1917, Pipp's bat hit enough homers to lead his league in that department, as well as setting the stage for future Yankee sluggers to dominate the baseball world in that specialty.

Another prominent hitter of that era, Franklin Baker, known as "Home Run" for his critical circuit shots in two World Series (1911 and 1913) against the Giants, departed the Philadelphia Athletics and signed with the Yankees. Baker's release was won via the deposit of $25,000 in Connie Mack's bank account, after Mack had experienced considerable difficulty luring Baker out of semiretirement. A standout third-baseman, Baker soon developed into that most incongruous of Yankee figures—a drawing card. Not since the days of Hal Chase had the New York team boasted of a player who could entice fans into the ball park. Baker managed to do just that—but not much else. He played six years for the Yankees, hitting ten home runs twice (an imposing total for those pre-Ruthian times), but his runs-batted-in production was much lower than his Philadelphia output.

With the signing of Baker and right-hander Bob Shawkey, also formerly with the Athletics, Ruppert and Huston served notice that they had something of a master plan for their team. They would seek headline players who they believed would seize the imagination of New Yorkers and win attention away from the perennial front-running Giants.

The idea seemed to be excellent, but the execution did not produce immediate results. In 1917, the Yankees slipped to sixth and in the process also lost many of their new fans. And they lost more than ball games, for Cap Huston, ever the vigilant patriot, and already instrumental in having drill sergeants assigned to all big-league teams, enlisted in the war in Europe. Soon he was in France with the engineers, and baseball no longer was much on his mind.

Before he left, Huston had been having disagreements with Ruppert on the subject of the next Yankee manager. Huston had been inclined to favor his old drinking and hunting buddy, Wilbert Robinson, once a Baltimore Orioles teammate of McGraw's and then manager of the Brooklyn Dodgers.

But Ruppert didn't cotton to Robinson, even if the Brooklyn team was often lovingly called the Robins, a shortened version of Robinson's name. The colonel, on record as saying that in "no sport can a man of means get the fun he will find in the ownership of a ball club," wasn't having much fun with Donovan, and he didn't anticipate that Robinson would be much fun either.

"I like you, Bill, but some changes have to be made," said Ruppert, as a prelude to Donovan's dismissal.

With Donovan gone, Ruppert then consulted with Ban Johnson about the managerial post. There were a few discussions with Huston by cable, but the case for Robinson wasn't pursued very strenuously. On the other hand, Johnson electioneered immediately for a scrawny little fellow named Miller Huggins, then managing the St. Louis Cardinals.

When Ruppert got to meet Huggins for the first time, he found it hard to believe that this man had been an infielder in the major leagues. Huggins had studied law at the University of Cincinnati, but this scarcely seemed to equip him for a leadership role. Only 5′4″ and weighing 130 pounds, Huggins looked as if he should have been riding horses at Belmont Park rather than riding herd on a platoon of surly ballplayers. But the hearty endorsement of Johnson, plus the equally emphatic support of J. G. Taylor Spink, the publisher of baseball's bible, *The Sporting News*, plus his own instinct about Huggins' integrity and baseball savvy, convinced Ruppert to offer "The Mighty Mite" the job as Yankees manager.

Within days the howling protestations of Huston, still fighting a war some three thousand miles away, could be heard across the Atlantic. He wasn't prepared to accept Ruppert's unilateral hiring of Huggins, so he continued to deluge Ruppert with explosive cables, even as he bombarded the press with angry comments. It wasn't that he was opposed to Huggins, so much as the fact he hadn't been consulted in the selection. Thereafter, even as Huggins would evolve into one of the brainy, compelling managers in the game, Huston never forgave Ruppert for what he regarded as treachery and duplicitous behavior.

The partnership, never too fraternal, thus all but broke down. In a matter of a few years, the two men would forever sever their business bond. As far as Ruppert was concerned, Huston's attitude bothered him not a whit. Huston kept fulminating; Ruppert kept planning to build his ball club.

Since he hadn't actually pursued the job to begin with, Huggins was not too happy with the situation. It was bad enough not to have many good players—now the enmity between Huston and Ruppert was also taking its toll, with Huggins caught in the middle. Despite this state of disaffection, the Yankees managed to finish fourth in 1918, a war-shortened season.

But Huggins hadn't yet been exposed to the full fury of Huston's temper. Returning to the United States a full colonel—a *real* one, in his eyes, as opposed to Ruppert's fraudulent title—Huston made life miserable for Huggins.

Huston carped constantly about the lack of progress on the field, invariably making Huggins the target. Nonetheless, in 1919 the Yankees wound up in third place, as they drew 620,000 fans into the Polo Grounds. This was more than twice the number they had drawn the previous year and only some 95,000 less than the Giants had attracted into the same ball park. It was clear that the Yankees, with the beleaguered Huggins, were headed in the right direction. The club even led the American League in home runs, serving notice that they would soon register a patent in this category.

In Roger Peckinpaugh at shortstop; Pipp at first; Baker at third; Ping Bodie, Duffy Lewis, and Sammy Vick in the outfield; Bob Shawkey and the misanthropic Carl Mays heading the pitchers; and Muddy

Ruel behind the bat, Huggins appeared to have the nucleus of a good ball club. With a bit more help from his friend Ruppert in the front office, Huggins believed he would have a club that might soon challenge for the lead.

Then two events in 1919, following The Great War, would shake the baseball world to its foundation. One episode—the Black Sox Scandal—almost destroyed the integrity and validity of the game. The other event restored and reinvigorated this American institution. In the process, the latter occurrence brought a remarkable dynasty to New York. More aptly, one might call this event a cataclysm, for it was the coming of George Herman "Babe" Ruth to the Yankees.

The owner of the Boston Red Sox, Harry Frazee, seemed to care more about producing Broadway plays than producing baseball winners. To back his theatrical investments, he was in need of a steady flow of cash. Frazee was actually a pretty shrewd baseball man—"He made more sense dead drunk than most people do sober," said songwriter Irving Caesar—but in trying to prolong the life of several Broadway turkeys, he had had to acquire a quick infusion of money.

Frazee reminded himself that Ruppert had money and a willingness to spend it. He also knew that in Babe Ruth he had a property that might end up solving his economic problems. Coming off a twenty-nine home run year in 1919, Ruth was blossoming into the biggest baseball idol in post–World War I America. The fact that he was also one of the best southpaw pitchers around also added considerably to his appeal.

In the off-season Frazee had gone to Ruppert for a loan of a half million dollars, primarily to sustain his show business dreams. Instead, Ruppert countered by saying he'd be pleased to put up a wad of greenbacks for the services of the twenty-four-year-old Ruth. After an exchange of views with Huston—who, in this instance, agreed that the Babe would be an enormous asset in a New York uniform—Ruppert pressed Frazee once more on the matter. No further urging was necessary for the cash-strapped Boston owner. On the day after Christmas in 1919, in return for a cool $115,000, as well as a personal loan of $350,000, Frazee agreed to donate his big pumpkin-faced kid to the Yankees. It was the mother of all baseball transactions, twice the amount that had ever been paid for a ballplayer up to that time. Almost a century later Red Sox fans still curse Frazee for making the deal.

Although the Babe was born in Baltimore to a saloonkeeper father who paid him little heed, then became a sensation in a Red Sox uniform, New York turned out to be the perfect stage for him. Here he would become a larger-than-life Yankee straight through the Jazz Age, the Roaring Twenties, and the Depression thirties. A myth-in-the-making when he arrived in New York, the Babe soon developed into the most implausible sports personality in history, a man-boy of extraordinary skills and voracious appetites. His homely, porcine features became more familiar than even Jack Dempsey's or Charles Lindbergh's. He soon lured millions of people into the seats. But more than that, he changed the way the game was played. In doing so, his towering home runs stole the headlines from all other great hitters of his era.

If ever a ballplayer was a one-man show, the Babe was it. He laughed, loved, fought, homered, bellowed, belched, drank, wenched, roistered, and cavorted, always untouched by any connection to reality and always with a seeming innocence that charmed millions. The quintessential rags-to-riches character, he delivered from the moment he set foot in the Yankees dugout. And it must never be forgotten that none of this would have happened to Ruth—or to New York—without the intervention of Colonel Ruppert and the damnfoolery of Frazee in the winter of 1919.

The fans wasted little time flocking to see Babe play for the Yankees at the rate of $20,000 a year, a monumental figure at the time but paltry compared with the salaries of contemporary ballplayers. In his first year at the Polo Grounds, as McGraw watched, more in anger than grief, the Babe batted .376, smashed an unheard-of total of 54 home runs, and drove in 137 runs. Such production moved the Yankees into third place.

Perhaps what bothered McGraw more than anything else was that Yankee home attendance zoomed to 1.3 million. The Yankees now obviously represented a valid threat to the Giants, both in fan appeal and in success on the diamond. It wasn't long before Little Napoleon—McGraw—abruptly demanded that Ruppert take his show on the road. The sooner the better, McGraw wanted the Yankees out of the Polo Grounds as tenants. Such surliness encouraged Ruppert and Huston to start looking around for a new venue for their franchise. In addition, Ruppert began to think of American League pennants, provided a few more pieces could be added to the structure. Again it was to Frazee that the Yankees turned.

First Ruppert pried loose from the Red Sox Edward Grant Barrow, whose middle name honored the Civil War general. Barrow was a hard-driving, fifty-two-year-old former journalist and baseball executive, who had managed the Red Sox to a World Series victory over the Chicago Cubs in 1918. But he had won renown primarily for reluctantly transferring Ruth from the pitching mound to the outfield, on the urgent suggestion of Harry Hooper, a Hall of Fame Red Sox outfielder. When Barrow resigned from Frazee's employ in 1920, Ruppert offered him the job as the Yankees' business manager, since he was aware that Barrow knew everything that had to be known about baseball and ballplayers. A physically imposing man fiercely committed to winning, Barrow knew the personnel of the Red Sox better than his own hat size. So it didn't take long for him to engage in further raids on the Boston locker room.

In the next few years, a steady stream of Red

Soxers came marching into New York. The group included Waite Hoyt, a handsome right-hander who had grown up streetwise in Brooklyn; southpaw Herb Pennock, with impeccable control and a patrician background; shortstop Everett Scott; catcher Wally Schang; and pitchers Bullet Joe Bush and Sad Sam Jones. When Jumpin' Joe Dugan was added at third base, the demolition of the Boston roster was near completion. Such personnel switches literally destroyed the Red Sox, even as they put the Yankees on the road to baseball supremacy. In 1921, the Yankees won their first American League flag, heading off Cleveland, as they won 98 games. In the World Series that fall, McGraw's Giants licked the Yankees in New York's first interborough Series. The two teams played a best-of-nine competition, with the Giants taking five of eight. The Babe had hit 59 homers during the season, although a badly swollen elbow limited his lusty swing in the Series.

The Yankees' distress at losing, even though they had been favored to win, was palliated by checks for over $3,500 to each player. The winning Giants received $5,265 each, by far the most money ever earned for World Series play.

Following the Series, the Babe, his fellow outfielder Bob Meusel, and catcher Fred Hofmann tried to cash in further by going on an extended barnstorming tour. This was in direct contravention of a rule set down by Judge Kenesaw Mountain Landis, who had been named commissioner of the sport following the Black Sox shenanigans. The Babe's anarchic behavior may have been generally condoned by the fans. But in a mano-a-mano with the judge, there was no contest. Landis fined the rebellious Yankees a sum that equaled

THE ABBREVIATED RIGHT-FIELD LINE AT THE POLO GROUNDS WAS A TEMPTING TARGET FOR BABE RUTH, SEEN HERE IN BILL PURDOM'S PAINTING OF A GAME IN 1922, A YEAR BEFORE THE YANKEES MOVED INTO THEIR NEW STADIUM. GEORGE SISLER, PLAYING FIRST BASE, FINISHED THE SEASON HITTING .420 FOR THE ST. LOUIS BROWNS. THE CARVED GRANDSTAND FACINGS DEPICTED, ACCORDING TO A CONTEMPORARY MAGAZINE ACCOUNT, "THE PERFECT IDEALIZATION OF NATIONAL MANHOOD AND WOMANHOOD." SHIELDS CONTAINING THE EMBLEMS OF THE EIGHT NATIONAL LEAGUE TEAMS ADORNED THE EDGE OF THE ROOF.

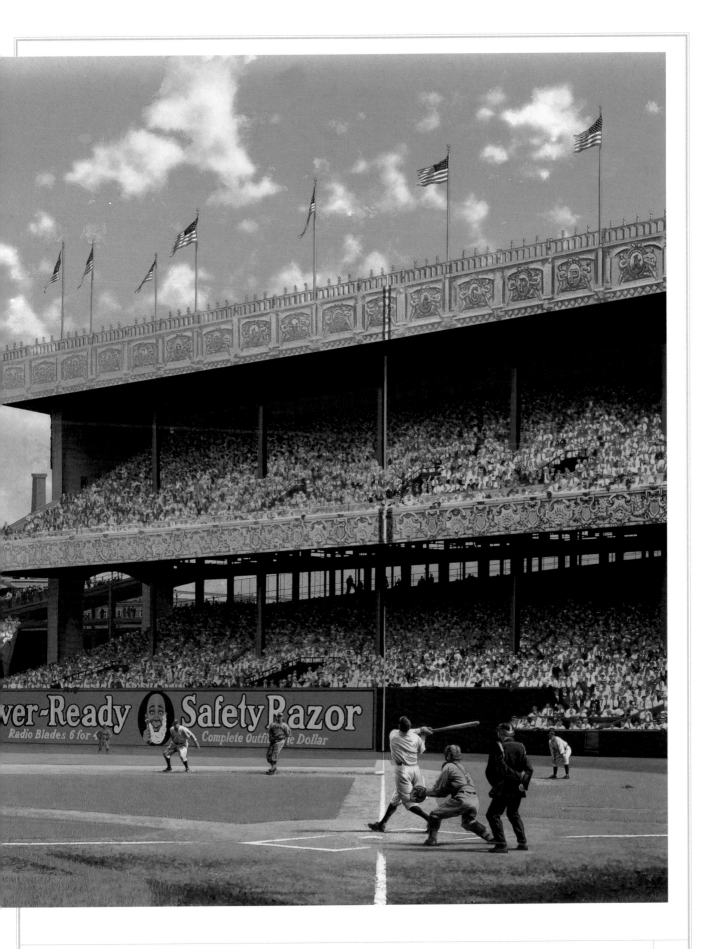

their Series shares and suspended them until May. Despite such punishment, the Yankees grimly held on in the pennant race. Ultimately, they edged out the St. Louis Browns, led by Ken Williams, Baby Doll Jacobson, and George Sisler, who batted .420, even though he was plagued by bad eyes. Ruth still managed to hit 35 homers, while missing 40 games.

Once again, in the World Series, McGraw had his men primed. Heinie Groh, of "bottle bat" fame, and Frankie Frisch, a local boy from Fordham, helped to down the Yankees in four games, one of only three times in Yankees history (1963 and 1976 were the others) that the Bronx Bombers have suffered such postseason ignominy. The Babe was stymied by Giants pitchers, collecting just 2 hits in 17 at-bats.

Huston was so angered by the Yankees performance that he informed Fred Lieb, a baseball writer who always seemed to be in the right place at the right time, that "Huggins has managed his last Yankee team!" This fit of pique told more about Huston's future than Huggins, for by the following spring Huston was out of the picture, having sold his interest in the club to Ruppert for an estimated $1 million. Oddly, he remained a director of the team, though nobody ever saw him again at a meeting of the directors. Most assuredly, he had nothing further to do with the fortunes of the Yankees, a grievous mistake on his part.

In spite of the Giants' romp over the Yankees, McGraw remained dedicated to the proposition that the Yankees should speed their departure from the Polo Grounds. He was convinced that the Yankees wouldn't be able to find a suitable location anywhere in Manhattan. He also figured that if the Yankees were forced to play on Long Island or in the Bronx, they would soon vanish from public awareness. But Ruppert did not play along with this scenario.

On the contrary, for some time he had been searching for an appropriate venue for his team. Since he owned the rights to Ruth's explosive bat plus the services of the other migratory ex-Boston players,

Ruppert knew he had to build a playpen large enough and dramatic enough to exhibit his performers. He was aware, too, that a bountiful postwar economy and an increasing acceptance of Sunday baseball underlined the need for a large ball park.

A lot in Long Island City was briefly considered by Ruppert, then rejected. He then eyed the Hebrew Orphan Asylum grounds in upper Manhattan. A contract was drawn up, and the deal fell through. Another plan scouted by Ruppert and Huston came right out of a futurist's handbook. It called for constructing a stadium or amphitheater over the Pennsylvania railroad tracks in downtown Manhattan. But the War Department intervened, despite Huston's excellent connections. It turned out that the space was to be reserved for anti-aircraft gun emplacements.

Such unsuccessful attempts frustrated Ruppert. But finally a nondescript lumberyard choked with boulders and owned by the estate of William Waldorf Astor was purchased by the Yankees for $600,000. Covering more than ten acres, the lot had once been a farm granted by the British prior to the Revolutionary War to one John Lion Gardiner. It was located across the Harlem River from the Polo Grounds, and ran from 158th Street to 161st Street on River Avenue in the western section of the Bronx, within easy spying distance of McGraw's troops. Judged to be an ideal site because of its soft granite bedding, as well as its accessibility to mass transit, the new stadium would be the neighbor of a subway that clattered by the site before submerging beneath the Harlem into Manhattan. Also, at the time the nearby Grand Concourse was considered every bit as fashionable as Manhattan's Fifth Avenue.

Under the aegis of the White Construction Company, work began on the stadium in the first week of May 1922. Within less than a year—284 working days—the edifice was completed. In short order, it became the game's most spectacular shrine, a summer meeting place for the worshipers, as well as an arena that could also be utilized for football games, boxing contests, and religious and political conclaves. Some suggested that the majestic establishment should be endearingly called "The House That Ruth Built." First to call it that was Lieb, writing in the *New York Evening Telegram*. But Ruppert insisted on Yankee Stadium, a name that has taken on universal resonance. A Yankee spokesman, speaking at the opening of the park, said that "the new Stadium would be made impenetrable to all eyes, save those of aviators."

The steel-and-concrete structure, with its massive triple-deck stands—the first in baseball history—featured 60,000 seats, about the same as the Roman Colosseum. Many Stadium crowds have numbered more than that, either because of flagrant misreporting or because of equally flagrant violations of fire laws.

Another pioneering innovation introduced at the Stadium was an enormous electric scoreboard, appearing in right center field. It not only featured the line-ups of both teams, with the continuing score of the game, but also provided the scores of out-of-town games in progress, as well as the pitchers involved.

Almost a million feet of Pacific Coast fir, transported via the Panama Canal, was needed to build the bleachers. Over 2,300 tons of structural steel, plus a million brass screws, helped to keep the game's finest showplace in one piece. Enough sod—16,000 square feet of it—was collected to convert the place into one vast farmland. There were 135,000 steel castings for the grandstand seats, and 20,000 cubic yards of concrete were added to the mix.

One obvious structural concession was instituted: a 296-foot right-field foul line, with a low fence. This neatly accommodated the Babe's southpaw stroke. In left field it was 281 feet down the line, while center field was a graveyard for sluggers who were incapable of pulling the ball down either line. At close to 500 feet, it was a vast, unexplored territory that seemed miles from home plate. Some critics did not feel that the Stadium's sight lines were adequate. Because of the size of the structure, many seats were far from the action and suffered from obstructed views. The towering stands also produced mysterious angles of sunlight and shadows that created problems for some players.

Of all of the Stadium's splendid components, however, it was the copper frieze, sixteen feet in depth and hanging from the roof of the upper grandstand, that became the most familiar signature of the ball park. Called on to draw up the plans for the Stadium, the Osborn Engineering Company, of Cleveland, who had rebuilt the Polo Grounds, didn't anticipate the widespread attention that would be lavished on their creation.

When the time finally arrived for the official christening, not a screw remained unturned and not a celebrity forgotten. On Wednesday afternoon, April 18, 1923, on a chilly day more suitable for football, Colonel Ruppert opened his $2.5 million palace for business. On the cover of the fifteen-cent Opening Day program were pictures of both colonels.

The Babe promised he'd do his darndest to commemorate the event properly. In the bottom of the fourth inning, with two men on base, he homered off Boston right-hander Howard Ehmke, a shot into the right-field bleachers, which would thereafter be known as Ruthville. This first Stadium homer was greeted with a roar that could be heard all the way to the Polo Grounds. "It would have been a home run in the Sahara Desert," crowed writer Heywood Broun. As the enormous crowd whooped its delight, the Babe carried his thin legs around the bases, at last touching down delicately on home plate. Then he raised his dark-blue cap appreciatively, before heading for the Yankee dugout. It was a ritual he had already patented and which he'd employ with panache until the day he left baseball in 1935.

The Yanks won, 4–1, behind Bob Shawkey. But that seemed less important than the fact that Governor Alfred E. Smith threw out the first ball and Commissioner Landis, exuding gravitas, took the subway

PREVIOUS PAGES: A SECTION OF THE RAMSHACKLE PROPERTY OWNED BY THE WILLIAM WALDORF ASTOR ESTATE IS SEEN HERE IN A PICTURE TAKEN IN 1921. THE TEN-PLUS ACRES BORDERED RIVER AVENUE AND EXTENDED FROM 158TH STREET TO 161ST STREET, IN THE WEST BRONX, ACROSS THE HARLEM RIVER FROM THE POLO GROUNDS. A PALACE WOULD RISE FROM THIS TRASH-STREWN LANDSCAPE. ABOVE: TAKEN IN THE LATE SUMMER OF 1922, THIS PICTURE SHOWS THE LOWER GRANDSTAND STRUCTURE, AND THE BEGINNING OF THE MEZZANINE AND THE UPPER DECK FLANKING THE THIRD BASELINE. BELOW: THE THIRD-BASE GRAND-STAND, VIEWED IN OCTOBER 1922, HAS ADVANCED CONSIDERABLY IN THE FEW WEEKS SINCE THE PREVIOUS PICTURE WAS TAKEN. THE FRAMEWORK FOR THE FRIEZE CAN BE SEEN ALONG THE EDGE OF THE GRANDSTAND ROOF. OPPOSITE: BY LATE JANUARY 1923, THE THIRD-BASE GRANDSTAND HAS EXTENDED TO ENCLOSE THE HOME PLATE AREA AND THE FIRST BASELINE. IN JUST A SCANT THREE MONTHS THE ENTIRE BALL PARK WOULD BE READY FOR PLAY.

uptown to the ball park. The attendance was announced as 74,217. Every inch of space was jammed, as the Seventh Regiment Band, led by the celebrated John Philip Sousa, serenaded those fortunate enough to have seats. The preponderance of folks in the crowd were men, most of them in business suits and fedoras or derbies.

"Governors, generals, colonels, politicians, and baseball officials gathered together solemnly to dedicate the biggest stadium in baseball," said *The New York Times*, which also added that 20,000 fans had been turned away from the spectacle. Later Ed Barrow admitted that since the Stadium had only 60,000 seats it was unlikely that 74,000 fans had been there. "It's only an estimate," he acknowledged. But whatever figure was accurate, it was still the largest crowd ever assembled for a baseball game (game five of the 1916 World Series had pulled 42,000 people into Braves Field in Boston, the previous high mark). By dropping the figure of 74,000 into the whirlpool of speculation, however, the club had assured the Stadium's mystique. From that time on many observers assumed the Stadium had been built for over 70,000 bodies.

The same afternoon that Ruppert and Ruth put on their inaugural show, a bulky, shy, twenty-year-old Columbia University student named Lou Gehrig was pitching at South Field on the Columbia campus, at 116th Street in Manhattan. In the course of this game against Williams College, Gehrig, who also played in the outfield and at first base for the Lions, struck out a record 17 batters before a handful of cheering collegians. Somehow, Columbia managed to lose the game. More significant was the fact that the bowlegged and perceptive Yankee scout Paul Krichell was there. He had been trailing Gehrig for some time. What had particularly impressed Krichell was Gehrig's powerful hitting, not his strikeout pitching. Some were already prophesying that Lou was another Babe, a crushing burden to impose on a young ballplayer off the streets of New York.

Within two months, Gehrig had signed his name to a Yankees contract. It called for a bonus of $1,500, a veritable Comstock lode for Lou and his struggling Yorkville family. Two years later, Lou would join Ruth in a symbiotic slugging relationship in the Yankees lineup. Batting fourth, behind the Babe, he became one

half of the most crushing one-two punch in baseball history. In June 1925, Lou entered the Yankee lineup in place of Wally Pipp, a pretty fair first-baseman himself, and didn't come out until May 1939, covering a total of 2,130 consecutive games and an output of 493 home runs (23 were with the bases loaded, still the all-time record). Only a dreadful disease named amyotrophic lateral sclerosis (later known as Lou Gehrig's disease) could cut down Lou's streak and halt his life at age thirty-eight in June 1941.

So the 1923 season had started out on a note of joy and triumph for a team confident that it deserved such

RIVER AVENUE
(JEROME AVE

a magnificent playground. Huggins' men proceeded to capture their third straight American League title, romping home miles ahead of Ty Cobb's Detroit Tigers. With an assemblage of fine players backing up the Babe, plus a pitching staff—Sam Jones, Herb Pennock, Joe Bush, Waite Hoyt, and Carl Mays—largely

ABOVE: THE OSBORN ENGINEERING COMPANY OF CLEVE-LAND, ARCHITECTS OF YANKEE STADIUM, INITIALLY PROPOSED A DESIGN THAT WOULD COMPLETELY ENCLOSE THE BALL PARK. ESCALATING COSTS, AND THE REALIZATION THAT COMPLETELY ENCLOSING THE FIELD WOULD CUT DOWN ON THE AMOUNT OF LIGHT COMING IN, PROMPTED RUPPERT AND HUSTON TO REJECT THE IDEA.

inherited from the emasculated Red Sox, the Yankees went on to face McGraw's Giants in the World Series once again. The Subway Series, as New Yorkers proudly dubbed it, aroused intense interest on Broadway as well as in the hinterlands.

For the first time, a live World Series broadcast was carried on the air, with the popular Graham MacNamee at the microphone, assisted by W. O. McGeehan, a sportswriter for the *Herald-Tribune*. The play-by-play could be heard along the Eastern seaboard. For those crowding the midtown streets of Manhattan, *The New York Times* erected a huge magnetic play-by-play scoreboard so Yankees and Giants fans could follow the flow of the action at Yankee Stadium.

With millions of ears and eyes focused on Yankee Stadium, school, businesses, and shops were depopu-

I was a little kid of about ten years old when I first went to Yankee Stadium with an uncle. We sat in the right-field bleachers, back of that chicken wire. One of the things I remember is that when a batter hit the ball, he seemed to be halfway to first before you heard the crack of the bat out there in the bleachers. I always thought that was weird. Years later, when I played for the Yankees, my mouth was still open at the enormity of the place. But it even seemed bigger to me, if you can imagine that!

**Phil Rizzuto,
Hall of Fame shortstop for the Yankees and longtime broadcaster**

OPPOSITE: GRANDSTAND SEATS COST A DOLLAR ON OPENING DAY. THE COLD WIND SNAPPING THE FLAGS MADE TOPCOATS THE UNIFORM OF THE DAY FOR MOST SPECTATORS. ABOVE: AN AERIAL VIEW OF OPENING DAY, SHOWING THE PROXIMITY OF THE SUBWAY LINE AND THE SLOWLY EMERGING BRONX NEIGHBORHOOD. FOLLOWING PAGES: ON OPENING DAY, PARKING LOTS WERE CARVED OUT OF THE MANY VACANT LOTS THAT SURROUNDED THE BALL PARK.

lated. Everyone played hookey to follow the game. In this Era of Wonderful Nonsense, baseball had truly become the most passionate obsession in the country. The front pages of newspapers reflected this concern: only a juicy murder or scandal could have robbed baseball, the Babe, and the World Series of its monopoly of headlines and coverage.

On Wednesday, October 10, in the first World Series game ever played at the Stadium, the *Times* fielded so many phone calls asking for the score that it was forced to shut down its beleaguered switchboard after the second inning. The game turned out to be a tight struggle, with the score standing at 4–4 going into the ninth inning. The first two Giants in the ninth were thrown out, bringing up Charles Dillon "Casey" Stengel, a big-eared, thirty-three-year-old outfielder who had been having difficulties all year with his shaky legs.

The left-handed Casey hit a meandering line drive that went between Bob Meusel, in left field, and Whitey Witt, in center. Before the two outfielders could catch up with the ball, some 450 feet from home plate, Casey was chugging toward third base, one shoe half-off. Meusel, considered one of the strongest throwers in the game, threw to shortstop Everett Scott, who then relayed the ball home to

catcher Wally Schang. But somehow Casey slid in safely, as surprised as anybody in the ball park that he had cantered to an inside-the-park home run. This astonishing feat, which won the game for the Giants, provoked a memorable literary effusion from that hard-boiled diarist of Broadway fables Damon Runyon, who, oddly, was born in Manhattan—Manhattan, Kansas, that is.

Here is the way Runyon described it:

> *This is the way old Casey Stengel ran yesterday afternoon running his home run home.*
>
> *This is the way old Casey Stengel ran running his home run home to a Giant victory by a score of 5 to 4 in the first game of the World Series of 1923.*
>
> *This is the way old Casey Stengel ran running his home run home when two were out in the ninth inning and the score was tied and the ball still bounding in the Yankee yard.*
>
> *This is the way—his mouth wide open. His warped old legs bending beneath him at every stride. His arms flying back and forth like those of a man swimming with a crawl stroke.*
>
> *His flanks heaving, his breath whistling, his head far back. Yankee infielders passed by old Casey Stengel as he was running his home run home, say Casey was muttering to himself, adjuring himself to greater speed as a jockey mutters to his horse in a race, saying "go on, Casey, go on."*
>
> *The warped old legs, twisted and bent by many a year of baseball campaigning, just barely held out under Casey until he reached the plate, running his home run home.*
>
> *Then they collapsed.*

Funny, but a player in those days was Old at thirty-three. Casey hit a second game-winning home run before the Series was over, adding insult to injury by thumbing his nose at the residents of the Yankees dugout. He was fined $50 by Judge Landis, though he insisted that his gesture had been misinterpreted. "A bee or a fly was bothering me," explained Casey, never at a loss for mischievous words.

Despite Casey's exertions, the Yankees emerged victorious in a six-game set, in the first million-dollar World Series in history. Over 300,000 people sat in on the birth of the Yankees hegemony in New York, witnessing the reduction of McGraw's club to second banana. Using his brain as well as his brawn and refraining from biting at curve balls, the Babe cajoled eight walks and banged three home runs.

"The Ruth Is Mighty and Shall Prevail" was the refrain typed by Heywood Broun, in an article for *The New York World*. How right Broun was—Ruth would prevail at Yankee Stadium for more than a decade.

In the next forty years, the Yankees would win nineteen world titles, a remarkable, unmatched record in baseball for sustained excellence.

Originally meant as a cathedral for Yankees baseball players, the Stadium soon had its charter expanded to include other events. One might have expected that the national hunger for blood would have been slaked by the dreadful violence in the trenches of the Great War. To the contrary, the fight game—with a platoon of colorful pugilists such as Jack Dempsey, Gene Tunney, Battling Siki, Harry Greb, Jack Sharkey, Georges Carpentier, and Benny Leonard—attracted a whole new neighborhood of strident supporters. In 1923, the Polo Grounds became the scene of five world championship fights, including a brutal brawl between Dempsey and Luis Angel Firpo, known as the Wild Bull of the Pampas. In just 237 seconds of fierce exchanges, Dempsey was downed twice (once out of the ring) and Firpo ten times. In the tumultuous second round, Dempsey finished the job.

OPPOSITE: COLONELS AND THE COMMISSIONER. YANKEE CO-OWNERS JACOB RUPPERT, ON THE LEFT, AND TILLINGHAST L'HOMME-DIEU HUSTON FLANK JUDGE KENESAW MOUNTAIN LANDIS ON OPENING DAY. ABOVE : YANKEE STADIUM'S FIRST FLAG RAISING WAS ACCOMPANIED BY THE SEVENTH REGIMENT BAND, WHOSE DIRECTOR, JOHN PHILIP SOUSA, CAN BE SEEN ON THE FAR RIGHT.

Yankee Stadium couldn't match Dempsey-Firpo for excitement that year—but in midsummer the Babe's big house was the site of its first boxing championship event, with Leonard, the lightweight titlist, dueling with a talented contender, Lew Tendler. Over 58,000 spectators, paying $452,648 (a record for a lightweight fight), watched as Leonard, a consummate stylist, won a decisive victory over Tendler, the son of a Philadelphia sweatshop tailor.

The ring was placed over second base, an area normally patrolled by shortstop Everett Scott and second-baseman Aaron Ward. As the fighters entered the ring, under the bright lights, with white towels encircling their necks, the crowd roared. It sounded as if Babe had just connected.

In ensuing years, the Stadium would become a showplace for some of the great names in boxing, including Mickey Walker, Mike McTigue, Young Strib-ling, Harry Greb, Joe Louis, Joe Walcott, Rocky Marciano, James Braddock, Archie Moore, Floyd Patterson, Billy Conn, Tommy Loughran, Max Schmeling, and Sugar Ray Robinson. Curiously, Dempsey, whose name became an eponym for raw power all over the world, only once exhibited his prowess in a Stadium ring. His two historic battles with Gene Tunney took place in Philadelphia and Chicago.

The Yankees were a strong ball club once again in 1924, but Babe's 46 home runs weren't enough to derail the veteran pitcher Walter Johnson and his Washington Senators, who won the American League flag for the first time. Still smarting from their World Series defeat at Yankee Stadium in 1923, the Giants, winning a pennant for the last time under McGraw, lost in seven games to the Senators in the Series.

Although they were expected to bounce back in

1923: A Year to Remember

In 1923, the year that Yankee Stadium opened its doors:

George Gershwin introduced "Rhapsody in Blue."

Bobby Jones won the U.S. Golf Open.

Pancho Villa, the notorious Mexican revolutionary, died at the age of forty-five.

Charlie Chaplin, Gloria Swanson, Doug Fairbanks, Sr., Dorothy Gish, and Rudolph Valentino were stars of the silent screen.

Ex–army corporal Adolf Hitler staged a Munich beer hall putsch that failed.

People were singing "Tea for Two," "Yes, We Have No Bananas," and "A Kiss in the Dark."

Jack Dempsey kayoed Luis Angel Firpo at the Polo Grounds.

Henry Luce and Briton Hadden started *Time* magazine, with the highest salary pegged at $40 a week.

Little Bill Johnston won at Wimbledon.

President Warren G. Harding died at fifty-eight and was succeeded by Calvin Coolidge.

The Philadelphia Athletics lost 20 games in a row.

An earthquake devastated Tokyo and Yokohama, killing over 100,000 people.

Abie's Irish Rose was in the midst of a long run at the Republic Theatre.

Baby Ruth candy bars, first introduced in 1920, were parachuted into the streets of Pittsburgh. Babe Ruth brought a lawsuit against Curtiss Candy Company, claiming they were using his name. Curtiss pointed out that the candy bar was named after Ruth Cleveland, the daughter of ex-President Grover Cleveland. Ruth was the first child born to a President in the White House. Curtiss won the case.

Argentinian Enrique Tiriboschi was the first person to swim the English Channel, from France to England, in 16 hours and 33 minutes.

SOUVENIR PROGRAMME

YANKEE STADIUM –
Opening Day
April 18 · 1923

COL. JACOB RUPPERT
President
New York American League
Baseball Club

COL. T. L. HUSTON
*Vice President
and Treasurer*
New York American League
Baseball Club

YANKEES
VS.
RED SOX

HARRY · M · STEVENS – *PUBLISHER*
PRICE 15 CENTS

ABOVE: THE OPENING DAY PROGRAM FEATURED THE GRIM COUNTENANCES OF THE YANKEE OWNERS. FOLLOWING PAGES: NEW YORK'S GOVERNOR AL SMITH IS THROWING OUT THE FIRST BALL FOR YANKEE STADIUM'S INAUGURAL. HE WAS OBLIGED TO REPEAT THE ACT SEVERAL TIMES FOR THE BENEFIT OF THE PHOTOGRAPHERS.

1925, the Yankees fell victim to an unexpected malady: "The Bellyache Heard 'Round the World." During spring training the Babe suddenly collapsed in Asheville, North Carolina, with some dire reports even stating that he had died. Rumors swirled that he had contracted everything from stomach poisoning to a venereal disease, neither of which would have been unlikely considering the manner in which he conducted his life. By the time he recovered, in June, the Yankees were in disarray and so was Huggins' temper. On a losing ball club, the Babe lost all interest in everything except swilling enough champagne and soda pop to sink the State of New York, not to mention his employers.

Late in the season Huggins confronted the Babe in a Yankee Stadium locker room redolent of liniment, soiled socks, and a seventh-place team.

Some ball yard!
Babe Ruth, in 1923

"Don't bother to suit up today," screamed Huggins at Ruth, who had again broken all records for arriving late at the ball park.

"For two cents I'd smack you in the face," Babe bellowed at Huggins.

"I'd lick you right now if you didn't have seventy pounds on me," replied Huggins, who didn't count very well.

When the brouhaha caused Ruth to be fined $5,000 by the Yankees, he roared in protest. But Colonel Ruppert and Barrow stood firmly behind the manager. At last, after much fuming, the Babe apologized, then returned to the lineup with a bang, hitting .290 by the time the season ended.

During the winter, the chastened Ruth broke down and cried at a dinner in which New York's playboy mayor, Jimmy Walker, about as ill behaved in his own sphere as the Babe was in his, delivered a maudlin speech in which he reminded the Babe of his duties to

The Big League Che

Photog
YANKE
As it ap
Recor

BEE

ILLARD'S
10 ¢
H-NU

the fans and to all those little dirty-faced urchins who rooted for the Yankees.

With no World Series in Yankee Stadium in 1925, a new commodity moved in—college football, at its highest level. With the college game came the dominating figure of Knute Rockne, the bald-headed gridiron genius from Voss, Norway, who abandoned chemistry teaching for football coaching and public speaking. Rockne had been guiding and goading the Notre Dame footballers from South Bend, Indiana, since 1919.

From 1913, the Fighting Irish, as they were called (even though the roster included a goodly number of Italians, Poles, Jews, and Germans), had been playing Army every year. The rivalry, growing more intense and nationally publicized each autumn, was staged in Brooklyn's Ebbets Field in 1923. The next year it was fought out at the Polo Grounds. At last, in 1925, it arrived, 'midst thundering hoopla, at its natural roosting

PREVIOUS PAGES: ALMOST FROM THE START, YANKEE STADIUM WAS ENLISTED FOR COMMERCIAL PURPOSES. A POPULAR CHEWING TOBACCO INCLUDED A VIEW OF THE PARK DURING THE 1926 WORLD SERIES AGAINST THE CARDINALS IN THIS POINT-OF-PURCHASE DISPLAY AD. OPPOSITE TOP: THIS VIEW OF THE GRANDSTAND TAKEN DURING THE 1926 WORLD SERIES DISPLAYS THE CONSTRUCTION THAT SUPPORTED THE MEZZANINE AND UPPER GRANDSTAND. OPPOSITE BOTTOM: BABE RUTH TAKING HIS CUTS IN A BATTING PRACTICE SESSION IN 1928. READERS ARE INVITED TO SUBMIT IDEAS AS TO WHY THE LOWER GRANDSTAND BEYOND THIRD BASE IS FILLED TO CAPACITY, WHILE THE REST OF THE PARK IS EMPTY. ABOVE: IN 1927, WHILE BABE RUTH WAS SETTING A NEW HOME RUN STANDARD, LOU GEHRIG, THE YANKEES' POWERFUL FIRST-BASEMAN, DROVE IN 175 RUNS AND CLOUTED FORTY-SEVEN HOMERS OF HIS OWN.

ABOVE: OPENING DAY, 1927, AND THE BABE IS FLANKED BY AN UNCHARACTERISTICALLY AMIABLE TY COBB, ON THE LEFT, AND EDDIE COLLINS. IT WAS THE FORTY-YEAR-OLD COBB'S FIRST YEAR WITH THE PHILADELPHIA ATHLETICS, AND HE FINISHED THE SEASON WITH A .357 AVERAGE, AN ACCOMPLISHMENT ECLIPSED BY RUTH'S RECORD SIXTY HOMERS.

place, Yankee Stadium. There, before 70,000 fans, on a rainy mid-October afternoon, Rockne's team defended a sixteen-game winning streak against the Cadets.

The proud, gray-clad Cadets did not parade at the Stadium that day, for by official dictum the corps was permitted only three football trips away from West Point's Plains, and they had already taken those by the time of the Notre Dame–Army game. Their supportive presence was not necessary, however, for the Army team overpowered Notre Dame, 27–0, for the most one-sided defeat ever inflicted on a Rockne-coached team. (The next year at the Stadium, Notre Dame reversed the result, winning, 7–0.)

Every year through 1946, the Stadium remained the site of the classic game. (The two teams fought to a 0–0 tie in '46, with $3.30 end zone seats going for $200.)

Unfortunately, Notre Dame–Army at Yankee Stadium became a problem. It evolved into an overhyped grudge battle, a Hatfield–McCoy dispute played out before 70,000 screaming zealots. Many felt the game simply got out of hand, as millions of unfulfilled ticket requests poured in every year. Even Yankee Stadium couldn't hold all that energy, all those boiling-over "subway alumni," all those uncontrollable beer drinkers. At last both schools reluctantly agreed to call off the spectacle. In 1947, Notre Dame got its last crack at Army, but the site this time was South Bend. The Irish won, 27–7.

In 1926, there was a "new" Ruth. The tongue-lashing seemed to have reformed him, up to a point. He crashed 47 home runs, batted .372, and knocked in 155 runs, as the Yankees rebounded to capture the American League flag. In the World Series that fall, everyone expected the New Yorkers to walk all over the St. Louis Cardinals. But the experts hadn't reckoned with a grizzled, thirty-nine-year-old pitcher named Grover Cleveland Alexander, once a farmboy in Nebraska.

The seventh and decisive game of that Series at Yankee Stadium was played on a cold, drizzly October Sunday, with only 38,000 shivering fans on hand. But they sat in on baseball melodrama that has been woven into Stadium folklore. The Yankees trailed the Cards, 3–2, in the last of the seventh inning. Two intentional walks to Ruth and Gehrig loaded the bases, with two outs. With the rookie Tony Lazzeri, second only to Ruth in American League runs batted in that year, coming to bat, Manager Rogers Hornsby of the Cards felt it was time to replace his veteran pitcher Jesse Haines. So he signaled once more for old Alex, the pitcher who had won the second game and then the sixth game, only the day before. In the latter contest, he had gotten Lazzeri out four straight times.

His oversized cap comically perched on top of his weatherbeaten head, old Alex shuffled in from the bull pen. Some insist that Hornsby peered into Alex's eyes before handing him the ball, for the pitcher was never one to pass up a postgame victory shot or two. Satisfied with what he saw, Hornsby put the critical assignment and the fate of the Series into Alex's care. (A dramatic footnote to the Alexander–Lazzeri confrontation was that both men suffered from epilepsy, although neither player apparently had ever suffered a seizure on the playing field.)

Three pitches later old Alex had triumphed. Tony

The sheer size of the stadium awed me the first time I saw it, when I was four years old, back in 1926. I had a tough time dealing with my fantasy, standing at home plate and facing Lefty Grove or Pete Alexander or whoever they dared throw at me, and digging in, to try to hit one out. Hit one out of this stadium, bury it in one of those far-off seats, almost beyond sight? Never, I thought, the stadium stilled my dream.

And then the Babe got under a pitch and the outsized thwack of his dark bat and the ensuing rainbow of white streaking across the sky not only told me I was witnessing one of those eventual 714 gorgeous home runs, but I also knew my dream still stirred. Sure, I said with the bravado of a midget left-handed hitter, sure I could hit one into the right-field porch. Just give me time!

Arnold Hano, author of _A Day in the Bleachers_

swung viciously at all three. The first roundhouse swing was a miss. The second swing produced one of the loudest fouls in Series history, the ball screeching for the left-field stands, then curving foul at the last moment. The third pitch sliced the outside corner, as Tony swung again and missed.

Overnight old Alex became a national hero and Hornsby was proclaimed a genius for plucking him out of the bull pen. Bob O'Farrell, the Cards' catcher that afternoon, never for a moment believed that Alex would fail.

"He was the greatest clutch pitcher I've ever seen," O'Farrell once recalled. "I gave him the signals on those pitches, but it didn't make any difference what the signal was. His excellent control was his greatest asset. Lazzeri would have had to have been Houdini to get wood on that third pitch."

It's hard to imagine the famous "Galloping Ghost," Harold "Red" Grange, serving as an anticlimax to old Alex, but that's what he was in the fall and winter of 1926. At the University of Illinois, Grange had rushed for 31 touchdowns in three years and monopolized college football headlines.

Grange completed his Illini career in 1925, joined the Chicago Bears, and participated in an arduous schedule of regular games and exhibitions. The next year, he left the Bears to play with the New York Yankees, a team in the newly formed American Professional Football League, a rival to the established NFL.

In Grange's first game with the Yankees at Yankee Stadium, 20,000 fans showed up, not too modest a figure for a budding league. After that, however, the crowds were neither large or enthusiastic. Only 2,500 fans paid their way in for Grange's second Stadium game. All told, for seven games at the Stadium, Red's Yankees drew only 116,000. He did better in later years, after returning to the Chicago Bears.

By 1927, the sports pages were cluttered with laudatory stories about the New York baseball team. "Break Up the Yankees," they warned facetiously. The Stadium became the home for "Five O'Clock Lightning," since games started in those days at three o'clock and game-winning Yankee barrages often got going at sundown.

The Yankees won 110 games that year, losing only 44. They grabbed one season's series with the hapless St. Louis Browns by 21–1. In every respect, it was truly a Roaring Twenties year for the New Yorkers, though the season had begun with on odd occurrence: On April 12, opening day at the Stadium, a fellow named Ben Paschal pinch-hit for the Babe before 63,000 astounded fans. Ruth told Huggins he felt sick, so Paschal went up for him and singled off Lefty Grove.

There were no weaknesses in the Yankee lineup. From the silver-haired leadoff batter, Earle Combs, through Murderers' Row—the Babe, Lou, Bob Meusel, and Lazzeri—there was no respite for a

pitcher. To this day many are convinced this Yankee team was the best ball club ever assembled. "There was never a team came crashing through like Ruth and the rest of the Yankee crew," wrote *The New York Times*' John Kieran.

Throughout the season of '27, the Yankees performed against a backdrop of publicized incidents that only served to heighten the long-running drama of the campaign.

When that other famous Ruth of '27—Ruth Snyder—was sentenced to die in May for the dumbbell murder of her art editor husband, the Babe and Lou were already caught up in their two-man home run derby. At the end of the season, Gehrig would trail Ruth by 13 home runs, with 47, but for a while he was hot on the heels of the Babe.

On the night of May 20 at the Stadium, 40,000 people gathered to watch a heavyweight fight between Jack Sharkey and Jim Maloney. As darkness descended on the ball park, Joe Humphries, the fight announcer with the voice of a circus barker, called upon the crowd to rise for a moment in silent prayer for the young man from Minnesota, Charles A. Lindbergh, who was flying across the Atlantic to Paris with only a chicken sandwich for company. The throng stood up, as if it were a single body responding to an electrical impulse. A great hush settled over the Stadium, as the many thousands bowed their heads and removed their hats. Sharkey knocked out Maloney in five rounds, but the hearts and minds of the crowd were with the airmail pilot in his tiny monoplane, *The Spirit of St. Louis*.

Just two months later, Sharkey, the Garrulous Gob, fought again in the Stadium. His opponent this time was the former heavyweight champion Jack Dempsey. There was a feeling in the air that the bout (which brought in $1,083,529, a record for a nontitle fight) might end the career of the thirty-two-year-old Dempsey, a dynamo that had burned out.

In the early rounds, Sharkey, eight years younger,

hit the Manassa Mauler almost at will, as Dempsey's classic stand-up style seemed made-to-order for Sharkey. Dempsey's face became a mask of crimson and one eye was closed. In the seventh round, Sharkey pummeled Dempsey all over the ring, with Dempsey forcing Sharkey into a desperate clinch. With his right arm free, Dempsey lashed several blows into Sharkey's body, causing Sharkey's face to turn the color of grass. Stepping back groggily, Sharkey motioned to the referee that he'd been fouled by Dempsey. As Sharkey protested, Dempsey crashed a left hook off Sharkey's unprotected jaw, causing him to sink quickly to the canvas. Many in the crowd screamed, "Foul, foul!" But Dempsey was declared the winner, setting off a loud controversy among ringside observers. The press was divided on the issue, but the verdict in Dempsey's favor remained in the record books, an unexpected and perhaps fromagenous knockout that propelled Dempsey into a second and last fight with Gene Tunney in Chicago in September of the same year.

By the time that shoemaker Sacco and fish peddler Vanzetti finally went to their deaths in a Massachusetts electric chair on August 23, the Yankees had amassed a 15-game lead. Ultimately, they wound up the season 19 games in front of the Philadelphia Athletics. It was rumored that Colonel Ruppert, who delighted in 20–0 blowouts by his team, was ecstatic.

The most exhilarating moment of the year, however, was the Babe's 60th home run, delivered on September 30, one day before the close of the regular season. On his road to the "sacrosanct" 60, Ruth hit his final eleven homers at Yankee Stadium, which must have pleased the ball park's architects. By himself, the Babe outhomered every club in the American League, while the Yankees hit 158 all told. (Curiously, August 1927 was the coldest August in New York history, some seven degrees below normal, perhaps accounting for the fact that the Babe hit just two homers at Yankee Stadium during the month.)

The Ruthian jolt arrived in the eighth inning of a

IN JULY 1927, AN AGING JACK DEMPSEY TOOK ON JACK SHARKEY IN THE YANKEE STADIUM RING, AND FOR SIX ROUNDS WAS PUMMELED BY THE YOUNGER MAN. IN THE SEVENTH ROUND DEMPSEY LANDED SEVERAL BODY BLOWS, AND WHEN SHARKEY GRIPPED HIS MIDSECTION AND CLAIMED A FOUL, THE REFEREE TRIED TO GET BETWEEN THE FIGHTERS. IT WAS THEN THAT DEMPSEY LANDED THIS LEFT HOOK THAT DROPPED SHARKEY FOR THE COUNT. SCREAMS OF PROTEST FROM SHARKEY AND HIS SECONDS WERE UNAVAILING.

2–2 game, off a southpaw pitch from Washington's Tom Zachary. Only 10,000 were there to witness the feat, since the game meant little to anybody who hadn't been tracking each swing of the Babe's bat. On two previous occasions in 1927, Zachary had yielded home runs to the Babe. But this was the home run everyone would remember and that Zachary would never forget. "Folks just won't let me," said Zachary.

"I came in with a good breaking curve and Babe belted it far up in the bleachers near the foul line. I always told Babe it was foul. He would swear and contend it was fair by four feet," Zachary added before he died in 1969 at his home in Graham, North Carolina.

What particular magic attached to the number 60? Why was there such a mystique connected to it? The Babe, after all, had hit 59 in 1921. So why the fuss over 60? Was it because he'd been the first man to hit 30, then to hit 40, then to hit 50?

Many members of the press seemed to exult in the achievement more than the Babe did. Twenty-four hours after the Babe had rounded the bases on number 60, Kieran pointed out that Dempsey hadn't been able to come back with his fists, but Ruth had been able to come back with his bat. "Supposedly over the hill, stumbling toward the discard," continued Kieran, "the Playboy of Baseball made a gallant and glorious charge over the comeback trail. . . . My voice may be loud above the crowd and my words just a bit uncouth, but I'll stand and shout 'til the last man's out: there was never a guy like Ruth!"

In the '27 World Series against Pittsburgh, the Yankees lived up to their press notices. They were simply too much for a Pirates team that had the Waner brothers, Paul and Lloyd, in the outfield, but little else. The Yankees swept four games in a row, with the Babe contributing two homers. But the pièce de résistance of the massacre was Pennock's masterful exhibition in the third game, before over 60,000 fans at the Stadium. The southpaw mowed down the first twenty-two Pirates who came to bat, before Pie Traynor singled in the eighth inning. Such a near-perfect performance was totally unexpected, for the Pirates were supposed to be death on left-handers.

"Yeah, that's right," said a journalist who had covered the Yankees, "but they're talking about left-handers in the National League. There's nobody like Pennock in that league."

As the Yankees again dominated the American League in 1928, with the Babe and Lou suffering scant diminution in their slugging output (Ruth hit 54 homers, although Lou dropped down to 27, even as he hit .374), there was one negative note. Pennock's arm was hurt, causing him to sit out the World Series against St. Louis.

But nothing could prevent another four-game sweep by the Yankees. Babe and Lou literally stomped on the Cardinals, gaining a measure of revenge for the 1926 defeat. In the final game, Ruth hit 3 home runs, even as he limped around the premises from an injury. Gehrig *only* managed .545 at the plate, against the Babe's .675. But the introverted first-baseman cracked 4 home runs, while batting in 9 runs, to complete the devastation of the St. Louis club. The Yankees were at the top of the world, after eight straight World Series games without a loss.

Notre Dame's football coach, Rockne, had always been a spellbinding locker-room orator of Ciceronian dimensions. But he reached his exhortatory peak in 1928, at halftime of the Notre Dame–Army game at Yankee Stadium. At that point, the Irish were in a 0–0 tie with the West Pointers. Reaching back to 1920, Rockne reminded his players of the deathbed utterance of the wondrous "tramp athlete," the twenty-three-year-old George Gipp, who had been the brightest of Notre Dame halfbacks.

"I've got to go, Rock. It's all right. I'm not afraid," Gipp whispered to him. "I have no complaints. Someday, Rock, when the team is up against it, when things go wrong and the breaks are beating the boys, tell them to go in there with all they've got and win just one for the Gipper." (Notre Dame then won, 12–6.)

Whether or not Gipp actually spoke such beseeching words (Rockne insisted he had, but Rockne could be artful and inventive), this pep talk became a chapter of American sports folklore. In the political arena, Ronald Reagan, who played Gipp in *Knute Rockne—All-American*, a 1940 motion picture, and a man who could be pretty inventive himself, made the Gipper part of his persona. He never missed a chance, after he became president of the United States, in 1980, to remind people of the Gipp legend.

There was still another big nonbaseball event at the Stadium in 1928. In July, Gene Tunney defended his heavyweight title against New Zealand's Tom Heeney. By this time, Tunney, the ex-Marine from New York's Greenwich Village, had evolved into a wealthy country squire, who delighted in his social relationships with literary icons like George Bernard Shaw. He appeared to have

PREVIOUS PAGES: THE YANKEES CELEBRATED A WORLD CHAMPIONSHIP IN THEIR FIRST YANKEE STADIUM SEASON, AND THIS PITCHING STAFF LED THE WAY. IT ALLOWED THE FEWEST RUNS, PITCHED THE MOST COMPLETE GAMES, STRUCK OUT THE MOST BATTERS, AND OWNED THE LEAGUE'S BEST ERA. FROM LEFT TO RIGHT ARE SAM JONES, JOE BUSH, BOB SHAWKEY, WAITE HOYT, CARL MAYS, HERB PENNOCK, OSCAR ROETTGER, AND GEORGE PIPGRAS. ABOVE: LATE IN THE 1928 SEASON THE LEFT-FIELD GRANDSTAND EXTENSION IS COMPLETE AND JAMMED DURING A GAME WITH THE ATHLETICS, THE YANKEES' PURSUERS ALL SEASON LONG. THE BRONX HAS GROWN RAPIDLY IN THE FIVE YEARS SINCE THE STADIUM'S OPENING. FOLLOWING PAGES: YANKEE STADIUM WAS THE SETTING FOR MANY EPIC FOOTBALL BATTLES INVOLVING THE WEST POINT CADETS. THE CORPS IS SEEN HERE MARCHING ONTO THE FIELD BEFORE THE 1935 ARMY–NOTRE DAME GAME, A MATCH THAT ENDED IN A 6–6 TIE.

only a minimal interest in his chosen profession, until promoter Tex Rickard arranged for him to fight Heeney, a plodding, dogged battler, who was known as "The Hard Rock from Down Under." As expected, Tunney delivered a sound thrashing to Heeney. By the eleventh round, with ringside spectators, as well as Tunney, doused with Heeney's blood, Referee Eddie Forbes wisely stopped the fight. It marked the last time Tunney ever stepped into a ring. At the age of thirty, he retired.

In 1929, there was little reason to suspect that all hell would soon break loose in America. But the whole structure of society soon came apart at the seams. The stock market crashed and, with it, the country's boundless optimism. Millions lost their jobs, banks failed. The Great Depression enveloped the land—and in the world of baseball, the three-year dynasty of the Yankees also came to an abrupt end. In the Yankees' home opener on April 18, 1929, against Boston, a new fashion wrinkle was introduced. It was the first time the Yankees wore numbers on their jerseys. Numbers were as-

signed according to the batting order. For instance, the Babe hit third and wore number three, Gehrig hit fourth and wore number four. Rud Rennie of the *Herald-Tribune* wrote that the Yankees, with large black numbers on their backs, "resembled an unusually tidy football team."

Curiously, at the start of 1929, rumors circulated that Gehrig might be traded. Why? To restore the balance of competition in the American League! Of course the notion that Colonel Ruppert would engage in such an act of equity was ridiculous. It turned out, however, there was no need for him to break up the Yankees, who had won six pennants in eight years. The Athletics—mainly through the pitching and hitting efforts of Grove, George Earnshaw, Jimmie Foxx, Al Simmons, Mickey Cochrane, and Max Bishop—did the job quite handily.

Over the next three years, Connie Mack's team finished first each time. The Yankees were hardly a basket case—they never ended up lower than third in those three seasons—but they needed more than Ruth and Gehrig to

overtake the Athletics, probably one of the best teams ever assembled.

To make matters even worse, at the close of the '29 campaign, a sudden, melancholy event cast a shadow over Yankee Stadium. "This team is tired," Manager Huggins said, one day in September. In reality, he was talking about himself. Within a week the little pilot, only fifty years old, was dead, from complications springing from an infectious disease of the skin. Many of the hard-boiled Yankees had had their difficulties with Huggins, but most of them respected his winning leadership. Even the Babe expressed his fondness for the departed manager.

In mid-July 1930, one of the strangest and most inconclusive heavyweight championship fights of all time unfolded at the Stadium. Jack Sharkey, a talkative twenty-seven-year-old former sailor, who had come close to knocking out Dempsey in 1927, faced the beetle-browed German Max Schmeling, the winner to be declared champion.

In an odorous finale in the fourth round, Sharkey was disqualified by Referee Jim Crowley for a low blow. Many in the protesting crowd of 79,000 expressed their discon-

I always sat in the right-field bleachers at Yankee Stadium, where the price, less than a dollar, was right. Thus my view of the Babe was always from the rear. His back, with the prominent number three emblazoned on the pin-striped shirt, generally faced me. In my snapshot of The Great Man, rarely did I see his tanned, friendly face, except when he occasionally turned to mug or grin at the fans or when he trotted out to his right-field position. I can still see those hunched shoulders, the curly, black hair peeking out from under the large-billed Yankees cap, the knickers riding high up on his knees, and the mincing celery-stick legs that mystifyingly carried him faster than anyone expected. To this day that remains my Ruthian image—the Babe, scouted lovingly from the bleachers.

Ray Robinson

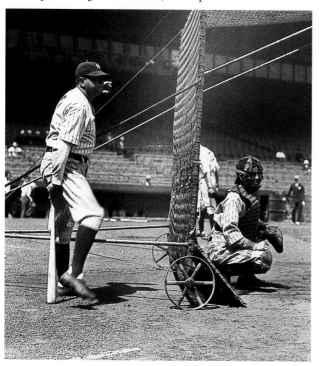

tent that Schmeling could wind up on the canvas and still be declared the winner.

That same Depression summer, as the Yanks tried but failed to make fans forget their empty wallets and stomachs, the former pitcher Bob Shawkey managed them. But he was ticketed to last only one year, for Colonel Ruppert had other ideas about what the Yankees needed to climb back on top. He cast a look at the National League and, in 1931, hired a lantern-jawed, forty-four-year-old Philadelphian, Joseph Vincent McCarthy, as his next manager, despite the fact that McCarthy had never played a single minute in the major leagues.

As manager of the Chicago Cubs, McCarthy won a pennant in 1929. A year later, he was fired. McCarthy was pretty good with the booze, but he never let that interfere with his baseball duties. He was all business on the diamond and seemed to have total recall of everything that had ever happened on the field. He was as colorless as the Babe was flamboyant. In time, his cold efficiency would be

OPPOSITE: Babe Ruth, awaiting his turn at bat during batting practice, in a picture taken during the 1929 season. ABOVE: Joe McCarthy, seen here before the start of the 1932 World Series against the Cubs, took over as Yankee manager in 1931. In his fifteen years with the Yankees he won eight pennants and seven world championships.

ABOVE: THE WEST POINT CADETS AND THEIR BAND ARE ON THE FIELD PRIOR TO THE 0–0 TIE GAME BETWEEN ARMY AND NOTRE DAME IN 1946. LEFT: ARMY'S JUGGERNAUT BACKFIELD IN ACTION DURING THE 1944 GAME AGAINST NOTRE DAME. FELIX "DOC" BLANCHARD (35) HAS JUST TAKEN A HANDOFF FROM QUARTERBACK ARNOLD TUCKER (17), AND IS OFF ON A FOUR-YARD GAIN BEHIND THE BLOCKING OF TOM "SHORTY" MCWILLIAMS (25) AND GLENN DAVIS (41). THE CADETS ROUTED THE IRISH 59-0 ON A GRAY DAY AT YANKEE STADIUM.

disparaged by some as "push-button managing." But he was a man who hated to lose and refused to coddle his players. He invoked rigid dress codes—jackets and ties in the dining room, please—and he was a stickler for physical conditioning. If he made rooting for the Yankees like rooting for U.S. Steel, as sore loser critics grumbled, he was still destined to remain around the Stadium for the next fifteen years. During that period, the Yankees won eight pennants and seven world titles.

At the start of his employment McCarthy's main problem was the overt hostility of Ruth. The Babe dearly wanted to manage the team. But behind Babe's back, baseball people hissed that if he couldn't handle himself how could he be expected to handle a ball club. Ruth continued to regard McCarthy as a second-rate pretender, so McCarthy decided the best way to handle the situation was to ignore the big man and develop amicable relationships with players like Gehrig and Bill Dickey. He simply let the Babe seethe privately without getting engaged in any public shouting matches.

So under McCarthy's deft hand, the Yankees returned to the winner's circle in 1932, just as the country was heeding the clarion call from the new president, Franklin D. Roosevelt. FDR had defeated Herbert Hoover, which should have given the Babe some satisfaction. Though Ruth was as apolitical as an earthworm, he had been criticized for making more money than President Hoover. His response, innocent as it was, had people chuckling for months. "I had a better year than he did," the Babe said—and nobody could disagree with that.

During the '32 season, as Jimmie Foxx took over the home run crown from Ruth, Gehrig finally engaged in a bit of one-upmanship with the Babe. Lou hit four home runs in one game in June against Philadelphia, at Shibe Park, something Ruth and

nobody else had been able to accomplish in the twentieth century.

But wouldn't you know it? On the same afternoon, John McGraw, the cranky old Yankee-hater himself, announced he was stepping down as Giants manager after thirty years and ten pennants. Bill Terry, at thirty-three years old, the best first-baseman in the game, after Gehrig, would inherit the job. The competitive ferocity had at last burned down in McGraw. For one last day, McGraw was the biggest news all over America. On Saturday, June 4, *The New York Times* featured McGraw on its front page, while Gehrig's feat was back on page 10, in the sports pages. On Sunday the *Times* didn't have a word about Lou's four homers, while several columns were devoted to "Memories of McGraw."

ABOVE: JOSEPH GOLINKIN'S PANORAMA OF YANKEE STADIUM IN 1937 SHOWS LOU GEHRIG AT BAT AND GEORGE SELKIRK ON DECK.

In the World Series that year, McCarthy extracted his revenge on the Chicago Cubs. The Yankees trounced the Chicagoans in four straight—making it twelve wins in a row in the Series. But all that anyone could talk about was the Babe pointing his finger at center field in the third game, then hitting a tremendous line drive deep into the bleachers. There are arguments to this day about the "called shot." Did Babe really signal he was going to hit a homer? Was he just mocking pitcher Charlie Root or suggesting that he still had one more strike in which to hit the ball? Whatever Babe was thinking or doing, the legend has grown, embroidered over time and adding to the Ruthian myth. Whatever the Babe did that afternoon, in his ultimate pantomime, it was only too bad that it hap-

pened at Wrigley Field and not at the Stadium. It was also too bad that Gehrig's performance in the Series—three homers, nine runs scored, nine hits—was totally forgotten. He had never been able to escape the bulging shadow of Ruth.

Over the next three years hard times caused attendance to plummet at the Stadium to almost half, though it still remained higher than elsewhere in the big leagues. The Yankees settled for runner-up each of those seasons.

By this time, the Babe's body was beginning to betray him. He hit 34 homers in 1933, then a dreary (for

In the early 1930s my Dad took me to Yankee Stadium. We saw the Babe throw a man out at second base and hit a home run. It was the greatest thrill of my life. After the game we walked across the field. The vastness of it was overwhelming. When I looked back I didn't see how anyone could throw a ball that far.

Lawrence Ritter,
author of *The Glory of Their Times*

him) 22 in 1934. Fat, fatigued, and close to forty, he appeared to have had his best days. As his team visited each city on the American League circuit, good crowds came out to see Ruth, many suspecting it was a last look at a legend. Late in September 1934, Babe played for the last time at the Stadium. All the while the Babe still nursed a burning desire to manage the Yankee team—if not the Yanks, maybe some other club would take a chance on him. But the Yankees front office couldn't wait for him to move out of the Stadium. They were more than willing to give him his release.

In the late days of spring training, the Babe was wooed by Emil Fuchs, the owner of the downtrodden Boston Braves. Fuchs, who had once signed Christy Mathewson to a front office job because Matty was an idol of heroic dimensions, regarded the Babe in much the same way. He also thought the Babe's presence in Boston could give a healthy jolt to the gate. So a deal was arranged for the Babe to join the Braves in the multifaceted role of player, vice president, and assistant manager to Bill McKechnie. After the initial euphoria wore off, it became clear that the scenario wouldn't work: Babe

OPPOSITE: YANKEE STADIUM IS VISIBLE ACROSS THE HARLEM RIVER IN THIS PICTURE OF THE POLO GROUNDS TAKEN FROM ATOP COOGAN'S BLUFF JUST BEFORE THE START OF THE 1937 WORLD SERIES MATCHING THE YANKEES AND THE GIANTS. THE BUSY RAILROAD YARD AND THE WATER TOWER WERE SOON TO BE DISPLACED TO MAKE ROOM FOR APARTMENT HOUSE CONSTRUCTION. ABOVE: THE CAMARADERIE OF BASEBALL, BOOSTED BY THE PRIDE OF PERPETUAL EXCELLENCE, IS MIRRORED IN THE FACES OF (LEFT TO RIGHT) BILL DICKEY, LEFTY GOMEZ, AND LOU GEHRIG. IN 1934, WHEN THIS PICTURE WAS TAKEN, DICKEY HIT .322, GOMEZ LED THE AMERICAN LEAGUE WITH TWENTY-SIX WINS AND A 2.33 EARNED RUN AVERAGE, AND GEHRIG LED BOTH LEAGUES WITH AN AVERAGE OF .363, 165 RUNS BATTED IN, AND FORTY-NINE HOMERS.

was exhausted and bitter and belted down too many drinks with Rabbit Maranville of the Braves.

There was a Last Hurrah, in mid-May, when the Babe cracked out three home runs in Pittsburgh's Forbes Field. The final homer, recalled pitcher Guy Bush, who threw the ball that Ruth hit, was "the longest damn ball I've ever seen hit, off me or anyone else. He got it off the fat part of his bat and there was no wind to help. And it didn't need no help, no way." Only 10,000 were on hand to see the last of Babe's 714 homers, a far cry from the roar of 60,000 people in Yankee Stadium.

On May 30, the Babe played his finale in Philadel-phia. Then, an embittered man, he quit the Braves. Until he died of cancer in 1948, the Babe would occa-sionally show up at Yankee Stadium, always accompa-nied by a hum of excitement and the fuss of the curious. He would hunch forward in his seat—often *not* provided by the Yankees—to watch his old teammates, whose names invariably seemed to escape him.

Now word from the West Coast was that a minor-league phenom named Joseph Paul DiMaggio was breaking down the fences for the San Francisco Seals. In one stretch, DiMaggio hit in 61 straight games, as he played the outfield with a silky elegance. Yankee scouts persuaded Ed Barrow that the youngster was worth $25,000 plus five players, despite reports of injuries that could hamper him. In the months before DiMaggio ever set foot in Yankee Stadium in 1936, the advance publicity about him was staggering. It was said that he had all the drive for excellence that Gehrig had possessed. When he finally arrived on the scene, he also proved to be as shy and aloof as Lou, yet there was an aura about him that caused people to wonder what he was thinking, even if, in truth, he may have been thinking very little.

Gehrig was the holdover from the wonderful team of the twenties, and still the captain, but DiMaggio, by acclamation, became the club's hope for renewed success. Subscribing to McCarthy's wish, Joe wore the Yankee uniform ("the surplice and stole of baseball," as Red Smith wrote) proudly. When he was asked in later years why he always performed in full throttle, he responded, in all candor, "There may be someone in the park who has never seen me play before."

With DiMaggio gliding in center field, an area that became a nightmare for enemy long-distance hitters, the Yankees embarked on an era unparalleled in baseball history. The team had pitching (Red Ruffing, Lefty Gomez, Johnny Murphy, Monte Pearson), slugging (DiMaggio, Gehrig, Dickey, Red Rolfe, Joe Gordon, Charlie Keller, Tommy Henrich), and fielding (DiMaggio, Frank Crosetti at shortstop, Gehrig, Babe Dahlgren, Dickey). They also had the much-maligned McCarthy deftly maneuvering the chess pieces.

In a fine freshman season, DiMaggio cracked out 29 home runs, while batting .323. But that was only a suspicion of things to come for the twenty-one-year-old. With DiMaggio usually batting third, and Gehrig coming up after him, the Yankees were a devastating ball club. They won the American League flag in 1936, then defeated the Giants in the World Series, although their twelve-consecutive series victories finally fell victim to the screwball master, Carl Hubbell. Coming off 16 straight victories in the National League, King

Carl won the opening game, limiting the Yanks to one run. After that, however, the Yankees literally bashed the Giants into oblivion. They triumphed in two games by lopsided margins of 18–4 and 13–5.

The following season, the Yankees showed the way to Detroit by thirteen games. They were inadvertently helped when Detroit suffered irreparable damage on May 25, 1937, at Yankee Stadium, before 15,026 shocked fans, when right-hander Bump Hadley hit the Tigers manager and catcher, Mickey Cochrane, on the head with a three-and-one pitch. Losing Hadley's pitch in the white-shirted center-field background, Cochrane went down as if he'd been shot by a sniper. The ball bounced off his head and back to Hadley on the mound. There were no protective helmets in those days and Cochrane hovered between life and death for over a week. When he recovered from the fractured skull, Mickey was forced to retire from an active playing career at the age of thirty-four.

In the World Series of 1937, the Yankes again faced the Giants. The interborough rivalry, so intense during the years of the Babe and McGraw, restored baseball glory to New York, once again the center of the game's universe. In the first two games of the World Series at Yankee Stadium, 120,000 fans watched the Yankees score astonishingly easy victories. The score was 8–1 in each game, a result that numerologists would have blinked at in disbelief. Only the freakily twisted left arm of Hubbell, in the fourth game, prevented a Yankee four-game romp.

The season had been a rousing triumph for DiMaggio, with his 46 homers (amazing production for a right-handed hitter in Yankee Stadium), .346 batting average, and 167 runs batted in. Gehrig was hardly a slouch, with 37 homers, 159 runs batted in, and a .351 average. He played with broken bones, the flu, lumbago, and other ills, adding to his Iron Horse reputation, and never appearing the worse for it. Dickey had 133 runs batted in, indicating that in

Championship Fights at Yankee Stadium

The name appearing first was the winner.

July 24, 1923: Benny Leonard vs. Lew Tendler

June 26, 1924: Harry Greb vs. Ted Moore

May 30, 1925: Paul Berlenbach vs. Mike McTigue

September 11, 1925: Paul Berlenbach vs. Jimmy Slattery

September 25, 1925: Mickey Walker vs. Dave Shade

June 10, 1926: Paul Berlenbach vs. Young Stribling

June 26, 1928: Gene Tunney vs. Tom Heeney

July 18, 1929: Tommy Loughran vs. Jimmy Braddock

June 12, 1930: Max Schmeling vs. Jack Sharkey

July 17, 1930: Al Singer vs. Sammy Mandell

August 30, 1937: Joe Louis vs. Tommy Farr

June 22, 1938: Joe Louis vs. Max Schmeling

June 20, 1939: Joe Louis vs. Tony Galento

August 22, 1939: Lou Ambers vs. Henry Armstrong

June 28, 1940: Joe Louis vs. Arturo Godoy

June 19, 1946: Joe Louis vs. Billy Conn

September 18, 1946: Joe Louis vs. Tami Mauriello

September 27, 1946: Tony Zale vs. Rocky Graziano

June 25, 1948: Joe Louis vs. Joe Walcott

September 23, 1948: Ike Williams vs. Jesse Flores

August 10, 1949: Ezzard Charles vs. Gus Lesnevich

June 27, 1950: Ezzard Charles vs. Joe Louis

September 8, 1950: Sandy Saddler vs. Willie Pep

June 25, 1952: Joe Maxim vs. Sugar Ray Robinson

June 17, 1954: Rocky Marciano vs. Ezzard Charles

September 17, 1954: Rocky Marciano vs. Ezzard Charles

September 21, 1955: Rocky Marciano vs. Archie Moore

September 23, 1957: Carmen Basilio vs. Sugar Ray Robinson

June 26, 1959: Ingemar Johansson vs. Floyd Patterson

September 28, 1976: Muhammad Ali vs. Ken Norton

ABOVE AND BELOW: ON JUNE 22, 1938, JOE LOUIS METHODICALLY DESTROYED GERMANY'S MAX SCHMELING IN THE FIRST ROUND OF THEIR FIGHT AT THE STADIUM, AVENGING HIS DEFEAT AT SCHMELING'S FISTS TWO YEARS EARLIER AND DEFLATING ADOLF HITLER'S WHITE-SUPREMACY PROPAGANDA.

addition to their other stellar components, the Yankees also boasted the best catcher in the game. By the end of 1937, the eccentric southpaw Gomez had a record of five victories, without defeat in Series play, tying him with Pennock, who left the Yankees in 1933, also with a perfect 5–0 mark.

As the Yankees hopscotched over the American League field again in 1938, with DiMaggio driving in 140 runs and Gehrig "dipping down" to 114, a transcendent event occurred at the Stadium. It had nothing to do either with the suddenly fading Gehrig or the inspiring performance of DiMaggio. It had everything to

The Iron Horse's Farewell

In preparing for Lou Gehrig Appreciation Day, to be held on July 4, 1939, some in the Yankee hierarchy speculated on the negative impact such a highly charged experience might have on Lou's physical and emotional well-being. Manager Joe McCarthy was concerned it could further damage Lou's health.

Despite such reservations, when the event was held it evolved into one of baseball's most memorable episodes, though, indeed, it was agonizing for all of those present.

Many of Lou's tough old squadron from the Murderers' Row club in 1927 were there, including Tony Lazzeri, Bob Meusel, Art Fletcher, Earle Combs (now a coach), Herb Pennock, Mark Koenig, Benny Bengough, Joe Dugan, Waite Hoyt, and George Pipgras, who was umpiring that afternoon in the doubleheader against the Washington Senators. Wally Pipp and Everett Scott, who had played watershed roles in Gehrig's career, were also on hand. Mayor Fiorello LaGuardia stood next to Postmaster General Jim Farley, who had started out life in upstate New York wanting to be a ballplayer. Eleanor Gehrig, Lou's wife of six years, sat next to Mom and Pop Gehrig, for Lou's sickness had brought them all closer together. The

54

Babe showed up, arriving late, as usual, and looking tanned as a lifeguard. Until this moment he hadn't exchanged a word with Lou for some years.

With over 62,000 fans sitting under blue skies to pay their respects, the ball games were all but ignored. When the first game ended, the Yankee players of yesterday, graying at the temples and in their street clothes, joined the current crew in a loose circle around Lou at home plate.

They listened as McCarthy, barely able to control his emotions, assured Lou, "It was a sad day in the life of everybody when you told me you were quitting because you felt you were a hindrance to the team. . . . My God, man, you were never that!"

When McCarthy finished, Sid Mercer, a veteran sportswriter, serving as master of ceremonies, presented Lou with gifts from his fellow players, from the writers, from the club's employees, from the Harry M. Stevens concessionaires—even some from the enemy New York Giants. Then he leaned over to catch what Lou, his face twitching and jaws contracting, was saying to him. Mercer stepped to the microphone and relayed the message.

"Lou has asked me to thank all of you. He is too moved to speak," Mercer said.

At that moment the chant "We want Gehrig, we want Gehrig" started to rumble from every corner of the big ball park. The fans who had come to pay their respects wanted to hear from their hero.

As he listened to the beseeching chorus, Lou drew a handkerchief from his pocket, blew his nose, wiped his eyes, and advanced unsteadily to the microphone. (McCarthy, fearful that Lou might fall, had whispered to Babe Dahlgren, "Catch him if he starts to go down.") His cap in hand, Lou briefly scanned the packed stands, now silent as if on cue. Then he began to speak:

"Fans, for the past two weeks you have been reading about a bad break I got. Yet today I consider myself the luckiest man on the face of the earth. I have been in ball parks for seventeen years and I have never received anything but kindness and encouragement from you fans. Look at these grand men. Which of you wouldn't consider it the highlight of his career just to associate with them for even one day? Sure, I'm lucky. Who wouldn't consider it an honor to have known Jacob Ruppert? Also the builder of baseball's greatest empire, Ed Barrow? To have spent six years with that wonderful fellow Miller Huggins? Then to have spent the next nine years with that outstanding leader, that smart student of psychology, the best manager in baseball today, Joe McCarthy? Sure, I'm lucky. When the New York Giants, a team you would give your right arm to beat, and vice versa, sends you a gift, that's something. When everybody down to the groundskeepers and those boys in white coats remember you with trophies, that's something. When you have a father and mother who work all their lives so that you can have an education and build your body, it's a blessing. When you have a wife who has been a tower of strength and shown more courage than you dreamed existed, that's the finest I know. So I close in saying that I might have had a bad break, but I have an awful lot to live for. Thank you."

With the conclusion of Lou's words the crowd let out a deafening roar. The Babe walked over to the stooped figure at the microphone and threw his arms around Lou's neck. The embrace was frozen in time by photographers.

Lou's valedictory has been acclaimed, without sarcasm, as baseball's Gettysburg Address. It's remarkable, too, that during the delivery, Lou showed no significant signs of slurred speech, often so characteristic of ALS.

R.R.

do with world politics, something that Colonel Ruppert had never contemplated when he built his baseball monument.

The heavyweight champion of the world, Joe Louis, regarded by Germany's dictator, Adolf Hitler, as an inferior human being because he was a black man, stepped into the Stadium ring on the night of June 22. Opposing him was Max Schmeling, one of Hitler's designated Aryans. Sadly, millions of Americans may have shared Hitler's beliefs about blacks. There were even well-regarded sportswriters of the time, including the revered Southerner, Grantland Rice, who wouldn't have considered inviting Louis for a round of golf.

In such an environment, Louis, beaten by Schmeling two years before, inevitably became the hope of America's black citizens. Thus, the match between

On a chilly Sunday in 1939, I went to see my first game of the year. The sports pages had been full of stories about Lou Gehrig. He was not himself, they said, something was wrong. The Yanks won with ease. But Gehrig was sluggish, he swung without power. Here was no veteran slowing up. His reflexes were so far off, you could not but observe the fact. I didn't know it was to be one of Gehrig's last games.
James T. Farrell,
from *My Baseball Diary*

these two men had social and moral implications rarely found in a sports contest. Schmeling, with Hitler's blessing, was confronting a man whose fists spoke for the ignored and despised. It was a startlingly prescient metaphor for the approaching war.

Demonstrating an explosive early assault, the Brown Bomber, as he was called, finished Schmeling in the first round of a scheduled 15-rounder. It took him just two minutes and four seconds to pound the bewildered German into defeat. Three times Schmeling

bounced off the ring floor, sent there by Louis's right-hand blows. The crowd of 80,000, full of Broadway celebrities and political power brokers, had paid $1 million, with tickets in the infield going for $30. They roared in astonishment, as Schmeling, seeking to become the first fighter to regain the heavyweight crown, was counted out by Referee Art Donovan.

"Max fell almost lightly, bereft of his senses, his fingers touching the canvas like a comical stew bum doing his morning exercises," wrote Bob Considine.

Louis fought with a fury he had never before displayed, for Schmeling was the only ring foe he truly hated. As he reaped $200,000 a minute, Louis made certain that Hitler got his message. "Even whites who hated blacks, but were patriotic and despised the Nazis, loved Louis for that," wrote historian Roger Wilkins.

That fall's World Series saw the Yankees whip the Chicago Cubs in four straight games, for their third consecutive world title. The result was a further vindication for McCarthy, as he turned in eight wins without a defeat in Series competition against a team that had rejected him. Ruffing was brilliant, with two more Series triumphs, Gomez took his seventh Series game without a setback (an all-time mark), and the Yankees hit five homers, one by DiMaggio. The third and fourth games at Yankee Stadium were viewed by clamorous full houses, which had become the custom in the Bronx park.

The one negative note of the Series was that Gehrig's performance was an ill omen of things to come: he hit four singles, without batting in a run, and batted fifth, behind DiMaggio, instead of in his customary cleanup position.

As the '39 campaign approached, it became sadly clear that Gehrig was in his twilight time. During the creeping mystery of his 1938 summer, something had gone radically wrong with Lou's body. There was lugubrious news, too, at the management level. Colonel Ruppert, the man who gloried in Yankee runaways, died in January, at the age of seventy-two. The reins passed to Ed Barrow.

In spring training, Gehrig often looked futile and uncoordinated. DiMaggio watched in gloomy fascination one afternoon as Lou missed 19 pitches in a row in batting practice. In the clubhouse, Lou fell down trying to put his pants on, and pitcher Wes Ferrell, possibly the handsomest man, next to Lou, in a big-league uniform, noted that Gehrig slid his feet when he walked. "God, it was sad to see!" said Ferrell.

McCarthy knew that something was wrong with Lou, his favorite player. But he still hoped that the Iron Horse might work his way out of it. When the season opened against Boston, Gehrig was in the lineup at Yankee Stadium for his 2,123rd straight game. On Sunday, April 30, at the Stadium, 24,000 fans saw Lou go hitless for the fifth time in eight games. Two days later, the Yankees were in Detroit. Like most of America, the Motor City was experiencing a pre–World War II cocoon of surface serenity and mass-produced happiness. But the sport was to suffer a wrenching body blow: After 2,130 consecutive games, Gehrig went to McCarthy and informed him he was benching himself for the good of the team. Babe Dahlgren, a fancy-fielding young man from San Francisco, was told by the manager to take over for Lou.

In June, Gehrig entered the Mayo Clinic in Minnesota for a battery of tests, which revealed he was suffering from the incurable disease of amyotrophic lateral sclerosis. In July, the Yankees held a day for Lou at the packed Stadium. Within two years, Lou was dead. He was just short of thirty-eight years old.

The Iron Horse was gone. But the greater irony was that the Yankees—with DiMaggio, Dickey, Charlie "King Kong" Keller, George Selkirk (playing the thankless role of successor to the Babe in right field), Rolfe, Crosetti, and the usual suspects on the mound, including Gomez, Ruffing, Bump Hadley, and Monte Pearson, as well as Atley Donald and Marius Russo— were still too good for any team to overtake them.

ABOVE: ALMOST A HALF CENTURY AFTER HE RETIRED, JOE DiMAGGIO STILL EVOKES POWERFUL MEMORIES. HIS GRACEFUL STANCE AT THE PLATE IS EVIDENT IN THIS BATTING-PRACTICE SHOT TAKEN DURING THE 1947 SEASON.

During this period, one of the rare moments of frivolity at the Stadium concerned the bout on June 20, 1939, between Louis and Two-Ton Tony Galento, whose "belly rolled like jelly," as writer Dan Parker described it. Nobody gave Galento much of a chance against Louis. In fact, one brave sportswriter, attending

Galento's training camp, yelled up at Tony, "You're nothing but a bum—and always will be. Louis will murder you!"

Galento yelled back, "I'm comin' after ya!" encouraging the sportswriter to start a retreat from the area. On his way out, the writer shouted, over his shoulder, "I reiterate, you're nothing but a bum."

Two-Ton seemed suddenly pleased. "I accept your apology," he shouted. Several days later, Louis kayoed Galento, the latest victim of the Brown Bomber's Bum-of-the-Month Club, in the fourth round.

have to play your best men," explained McCarthy, mischievously. DiMaggio hit a home run, as the American League—that is, the Yankees—beat the National League 3–1, before over 63,000 people.

At the end of the year, the Yankees had won 106 games, leaving the Red Sox in the mist, 17 games behind. In the World Series, a good Cincinnati team, whose two right-handed pitchers, Paul Derringer and Bucky Walters, had won 52 games between them, simply couldn't cope with Yankee home run power. Keller had an enormously productive series, hitting three of seven Yankee home runs and six RBIs. Humming the same old tune, the New Yorkers swept the Series in four straight, to become the first team ever to win four consecutive world titles, as well as four consecutive American League flags.

It looked as if nothing short of a locomotive crash could put an end to the remarkable Yankee hegemony. This was especially true because the team was nourished by a farm system, principally clubs in Newark and Kansas City, that constantly coughed up talented young players. Run by George Weiss, who had been hired by Barrow eight years before, the Yankees' farm operation was inspired by the St. Louis Cardinals' system, created by that shrewd pioneer Branch Rickey. (Rickey was not through pioneering, for in later years

In July, the All-Star Game was played at Yankee Stadium for the first time, as New York was awarded the annual contest as part of the celebration of the World's Fair. McCarthy, who despised failure, loaded the American League starting lineup with six of his players, including the starting pitcher, Ruffing. "You

ABOVE LEFT; JOE DiMAGGIO, IN THE MIDST OF HIS FIFTY-SIX-GAME HITTING STREAK IN 1941, IS SEEN HERE RAPPING OUT A SINGLE AGAINST THE WASHINGTON SENATORS.

he brought Jackie Robinson into the game, to break down the infamous color barrier.)

McCarthy had high expectations in 1940. He was confident that his team could win for a fifth straight time. But the Yankees proved themselves human after all. Even DiMaggio's league-leading .352 average was not sufficient to bring the Yankees another pennant. The seemingly rubber-armed Gomez ran out of gas, with a 3–3 record, and several hitters experienced off years. It added up to a third-place finish, two games behind Detroit in first, scarcely a tragedy but a temporary halt in the assembly-line efficiency of McCarthy's club.

In the summer of 1941, in the waning days of the Great Depression, still another imperishable Yankee legend was born. As a devastating world war gathered steam, DiMaggio had become the preeminent Yankee in a lineup dotted with high achievers. In his five years with New York, he had performed with such smooth competence that he was even able to talk the hard-crusted Barrow into annual pay raises.

Now twenty-six years old, at 6'2″ and 200 pounds, lean and long-legged, DiMaggio had developed a magisterial manner that attracted even as it rebuffed. There were times when he could be as chilly as a Vermont landscape. But despite his aloofness, DiMaggio had already become one of the most charismatic sports figures of his era, in a baseball time already glutted with dominating personalities. In his own American League Joe had to compete with Ted Williams, Boston's splendid batting machine, and Bob Feller, possibly the fastest-throwing pitcher of all time. In the other league, over at Brooklyn's Ebbets Field, young Pete Reiser was positively heroic as he constantly challenged the outfield fences with his body.

Outside of baseball, there were other giants: the patrician president of the United States, Franklin D. Roosevelt, inventor and master of the fireside chat; Winston Churchill, with a bulldog grasp on the British psyche; New York City's tiny buzzsaw of a mayor, Fiorello LaGuardia; Clark Gable, every woman's nominee for lover and boyfriend; Bing Crosby, that most casual of crooners; and macho author Ernest Hemingway, who would later write DiMaggio into his fiction.

At the outset of the 1941 season, DiMaggio hit in eight straight games. Batting over .500 at this stage, Joe seemed as much of an overmatch against American League pitchers as Hitler's Luftwaffe was against Britain's undermanned RAF. Then, inexplicably, DiMaggio went into a slump, and his average plummeted.

On May 15, on a flypaper-sticky day, as 9,040 looked on at Yankee Stadium, the White Sox blasted the Yankees, 13–1. Batting fourth, DiMaggio singled against southpaw Ed Smith. Nobody knew it at the time, but baseball's most revered streak had begun. Over the next ten contests, all at Yankee Stadium, DiMaggio hit safely in each game.

Through May and early June, DiMaggio's tapestry of consistency rolled on. The days were also filled with speculation about Hitler's associate, Rudolf Hess, whose strange aerial adventure took him to Scotland. There were reports, too, that Max Schmeling had been killed in action in Crete trying to flee capture by the British. And DiMaggio's rival, Hank Greenberg of the Detroit Tigers, put in the first days of his military basic training.

Soon Joe's quotidian efforts were celebrated in Alan Courtney's song lyrics, "Joe, Joe DiMaggio, we want you on our side." On Monday, June 2, Joe connected for two hits off the great Feller in Cleveland, as he moved one-third of the way toward an achievement that was captivating America. That night, Gehrig, just short of his thirty-eighth birthday, died in his sleep at Riverdale, in the Bronx.

A one-hopper over White Sox shortstop Luke Appling's head on June 17 pushed the streak to 30 games, an all-time Yankees mark. The next night, Joe Louis

retained his heavyweight title at the Polo Grounds by kayoing the converted light heavyweight Billy Conn in the thirteenth round.

On July 1, at the stadium, before a midweek crowd of over 52,000, DiMaggio tied the mark of the Baltimore Orioles' Wee Willie Keeler at 44, as he hit in both games of a doubleheader against the Red Sox. "For the fans there was no escape from the magnetic force that drew them to their radios to hear the announcer report the grim but still dreamlike news of the war in Europe and then, at some point in the program, add, 'and Joe DiMaggio got his hit today to extend . . . ,'" Dave Anderson has written. Each morning, along with the toast and coffee, went the ritual question "How did Joe do?"

Lou Gehrig's centerfield monument was unveiled at Yankee Stadium on July 6, as 66,000 fans sat in on the ceremony. DiMaggio once again came through for his audience, as he propelled six hits in a doubleheader with Philadelphia. The streak was now at 48. Number 50 followed on July 11, as DiMaggio whacked St. Louis pitching for four hits. At this point, Joe was on a spree of 16 hits in 25 at-bats. As war clouds grew more ominous, Joe's bat got hotter.

The streak moved to 53 on July 13, before 50,387 in Chicago's Comiskey Park, the largest crowd at that stadium since the All-Star Game inaugural in 1933. The next day, DiMaggio lifted the streak to 54, with a lucky hit through the White Sox infield. On the same day, a Hollywood producer revealed he would film the life story of Lou Gehrig. One of those mentioned to play Lou's role was the former sportscaster and Grade-B actor Ronald Reagan. Gary Cooper eventually signed for the part, and the Babe agreed to play himself.

On July 15, DiMaggio pushed the streak to 55 against Ed Smith, the White Sox pitcher he had faced when he began his historic barrage two months before. That same afternoon Harold Ickes, Roosevelt's curmudgeonly Secretary of the Interior, characterized another American hero, Charles Lindbergh, as "the Knight of the German Eagle," for suggesting that Hitler's Germany couldn't be beaten in a war.

The next day, in Cleveland, Joe banged out three hits, to advance to 56 straight games. On July 17, the following night, a roaring crowd of 68,000 showed up to root for Cleveland's home team, and for Joe, at the same time. But ill fortune finally turned against him. On two attempts, Joe hit vicious line drives that wound up in third-baseman Ken Keltner's glove. On his last at-bat, Joe hit one up the middle that shortstop Lou Boudreau turned into a double play.

The long streak—29 games were at Yankee Stadium, 27 on the road—had ended. "I wanted it to go on forever," said DiMaggio, as he puffed on his inevitable Camel after the game.

DiMaggio went on another tear of 16 games after he was stopped on July 17. If Keltner hadn't barred the way, DiMaggio's streak would have gone to 73! Less than six months later, the Japanese attacked the Hawaiian island of Oahu, a place few Americans had ever heard of. The sneak assault cost 2,280 American lives and 1,109 wounded. "The day of infamy," as President Roosevelt called December 7, 1941, had brought the United States into World War II.

By that fall, the Yankees had won the American League pennant for the twelfth time. They were helped considerably by a tiny rookie shortstop, Phil Rizzuto, who lasted for fifteen years as a player, then became a permanent presence in the Yankees' TV and radio booth. The Scooter, as Rizzuto was affectionately called, added the exclamation "Holy Cow" to the language of baseball broadcasting.

The World Series foe in 1941 for the Yankees turned out to be the Brooklyn Dodgers, survivors of a torrid National League pennant race with the Cardinals. The Dodgers were managed by Leo Durocher, who in the early tumultuous days of his career had played shortstop for the Yankees. Flaunting a strident, profane, wise guy personality, Durocher had rubbed the Babe the wrong way, and many of his traits were adopted by his Brooklyn players. The last time Brooklyn had won a flag had been 1920, so the natives of the borough were at fever pitch to knock off their elitist Bronx rivals.

After three tightly pitched games, the Yankees led, two games to one. But it was the fourth game, at Ebbets Field, that will forever live in the memory of the 34,000 Dodgers fans who were there, as well as the millions who were tuned in to Red Barber's words. Going into the ninth inning, the Dodgers led, 4–3. Hugh Casey, a hard-throwing, durable relief pitcher for Brooklyn, retired the first two Yankees in the top of the ninth. Casey appeared well on the way to victory, which would tie the Series at two-all, and to a well-merited shower. But he was to earn only the shower.

With three balls and two strikes on him, Tommy Henrich swung mightily at the next pitch—and missed. But Dodgers catcher Mickey Owen missed, too. The "third" strike skidded past him, rolling to the grandstand. Henrich sped to first and was safe. Then came the deluge. The new life for Henrich proved to be the ruination of the despondent Casey. The Yankees staged a last-minute rally to score four runs and win the game. The demoralized Dodgers were dead. Ordinarily a fine defensive catcher, Owen was anointed the goat for permitting the ball to get past him. Later, he publicly kicked himself, not for the misplay but for not calling time.

"I should have stopped the game at that point," Owen said, "to give Casey and myself a chance to get over the shock and surprise. That might have cooled off the Yankees." Overlooked in the high drama of the errant pitch was the Yankees' ability to sustain a rally that was so typical of McCarthy's men.

With the coming of the war years, the Yankees, at the beginning not hit hard by military inductions, managed to retain their supremacy.

A plan was worked out for the Army and Navy Re-

When I made my first visit to the Bronx ball yard in 1942, I was not yet a teenager. But one thing I already was–a baseball romancer, fascinated by the game's history. I was also a Brooklyn Dodgers fan, sitting there in the home of the team that had humiliated my heroes the previous autumn, hoping that the visitors–in this case, Cleveland–would do them some damage. But deeper purities also made their presence felt. It was, first, the size of the place. How many Ebbets Fields could you have fit in there? Left field seemed, from my grandstand seat behind first base, to extend almost to the suburbs of Albany, while center field seemed absolutely imperial in its expanse. I confess looking around at those thousands of Yankee fans surrounding me–none of whom, it seemed, were suffering the anxieties of winning or losing that I always noted among my fellow Dodger fans at Ebbets Field–and envying them being shareholders in all of this imperious history, this glory, this stadium. When I returned home that evening, my father asked me what I thought of Yankee Stadium.

"I still like Ebbets Field," I said. But that wasn't what he meant.
Donald Honig, baseball historian and novelist

lief Fund to receive the proceeds from one home game of each ball club. Yankee Stadium, as the largest park of them all, was the stage for an August 23 Sunday doubleheader with Washington, at which almost 70,000 fans paid $80,000 into the coffers of the fund.

Most of the people who came that afternoon in 1942 were there to watch the Babe, now forty-seven and plump as a pumpkin, confront the supreme strike-out pitcher, Walter Johnson, fifty-five, in a between-

PREVIOUS PAGES: A SHIRT-SLEEVE CROWD JAMS THE CENTER-FIELD BLEACHERS FOR A HOLIDAY DOUBLEHEADER IN 1942. ABOVE: AUXILIARY FIELD-LEVEL SCOREBOARDS WERE ADDED IN RIGHT AND LEFT FIELD FOR THE 1946 SEASON. LEFT: YANKEE HOME-OPENER CELEBRATIONS ON APRIL 30, 1946, WERE DOUSED BY BOB FELLER, SEEN HERE FIRING AWAY AT JOE DiMAGGIO. FELLER PITCHED A 1–0 NO-HITTER. THE ONLY RUN WAS SCORED BY FELLER'S CATCHER, FRANKIE HAYES, WHO HIT A HOME RUN IN THE TOP OF THE NINTH INNING. ED ROMMEL IS THE UMPIRE. OPPOSITE TOP: THE FIRST NIGHT GAME AT YANKEE STADIUM WAS PLAYED ON MAY 28, 1946. THE YANKEES LOST TO THE SENATORS 2–1. OPPOSITE BOTTOM: YANKEE STADIUM WAS THE SETTING FOR MANY EPIC BOXING MATCHES BEFORE THE ERA OF CLOSED-CIRCUIT TELEVISION. THIS PICTURE WAS TAKEN DURING THE JOE LOUIS–BILLY CONN BOUT IN JUNE 1946, A FIGHT THAT LOUIS WAS HARD PRESSED TO WIN.

the-games exhibition. Neither man had prepared much for this theatrical mano-a-mano. Johnson said he hadn't thrown a ball in a half dozen years, and the Babe had done his training at the supper table and on the golf course. Johnson threw several warmup tosses to Benny Bengough, the former Yankees catcher, now a coach with Washington, before the Babe stepped in against him.

On the fifth pitch from Johnson, the Babe connected for a line drive into the right-field seats, at the 296-foot mark. Following that there were several fouls. Then the Babe unloaded a majestic fly ball that soared

into the upper deck in right. It was on Johnson's twentieth pitch, and it veered foul by a few feet. As the crowd roared, Ruth decided to end the act right there. He jogged slowly around the bases, as Johnson and the audience watched appreciatively. It marked the last time the two Hall of Famers ever appeared together on a ball field. Johnson died four years later, and Ruth's life ended in 1948.

In the 1942 World Series against St. Louis, the highly favored New Yorkers were upset in four straight games, after winning the first game behind Ruffing. In the final game, the Cards' Whitey Kurowski hit a game-winning, ninth-inning homer, as 70,000 watched at the Stadium on a brilliant October afternoon. It marked the first loss for the Yankees in a Series since the Cards had edged them in 1926.

With a roster still good enough to win—even with DiMaggio, Rizzuto, Henrich, and Ruffing gone—the Yankees beat the Cards in the 1943 World Series. The St. Louis team boasted Stan Musial, shortstop Marty Marion, the Cooper brothers, pitcher Mort and catcher Walker, and Harry "The Cat" Brecheen. In the first three games at Yankee Stadium close to 70,000 were in attendance for each contest, a remarkable showing during wartime.

With the war still raging in 1944 and 1945, the Yankees fielded a team that was almost unrecognizable, although their second-baseman, George Stirnweiss, led the American League in batting, with a puny .309 mark, in '45. By this time most front-rank players were serving their country, even though baseball, encouraged by a green light from the Roosevelt White House, never faced a shutdown, as it had in World War I.

There were no pennant victories for McCarthy in either year—and remarkably, the downtrodden St. Louis Browns won the pennant in 1944.

The big news for the Yankees in the winter of 1945 came from off the diamond. The heirs of Colonel Ruppert—Helen Wyant, Mrs. J. Basil Maguire, and Mrs. Joseph Holleran—announced that they'd sold their interests in the ball club for $2,800,000 to a triumvirate. Heading this group was the colorful and unpredictable Leland Stanford "Larry" MacPhail, a true baseball innovator, when he wasn't drinking too much. When he headed the Cincinnati Reds in the 1930s, MacPhail brought night ball to that Ohio city. A few years later he energized the Brooklyn franchise, staying around long enough to produce a winner, as well as the introduction of night ball. With a war to be fought, he picked off a commission as a lieutenant colonel, thus adding to an already vibrant legend. He was, after all, the man who supposedly kidnapped the Kaiser in World War I.

One of the other new owners of the Yankees was the millionaire Dan Topping, who was constantly referred to in the tabloids as a "playboy sportsman." When he wasn't playboying, Topping was also owner of the Brooklyn pro football franchise and an army captain. Del Webb, the third man in the mix, was an Arizona construction magnate.

It was clear that the baseball-oriented MacPhail would be calling the shots—and that's exactly what he did. He was determined to modernize and streamline the postwar Yankees. Lights were finally installed in the big ball park, even as some grumpy traditionalists begged to disagree, and the first night game was played on May 28, 1946. (When it was discovered during World War II that the lights of Ebbets Field and the Polo Grounds revealed ships in New York harbor at night, the Yankees chose to postpone construction of their own lighting system.) MacPhail also built a plush Stadium club behind the grandstand, with a box-seat plan that charged up to $600 for four seats. For the first time, too, MacPhail, with the instincts of a P. T. Barnum, staged fashion shows and track and field events, all of which set the turnstiles humming. In 1946, a record 2,265,512 fans flocked to the Stadium, a number far surpassing all previous Yankee figures.

Most of the prewar players—including DiMaggio, Keller, and Henrich—were back in 1946, but by May McCarthy had suffered enough from MacPhail's intrusions. The manager quit and went home to his upstate farm, after fifteen years at the helm. The popular longtime catcher Bill Dickey, once Gehrig's roommate, took over the club. He resigned late in the season, realizing that his temperament wasn't quite up to the job. Johnny Neun replaced him. Three Yankee managers in one season was another club record, albeit a discordant one.

That summer the one promotion that failed to attract another enormous crowd to the Stadium was a rerun of the Joe Louis–Billy Conn fight of 1941. Louis had emerged from the army four years older and bankrupt. Promoter Mike Jacobs thought he had just the solution for Joe's financial condition, and of course his own. Figuring that a war-fatigued nation was hungry for a dream rematch between these two pugilists, Jacobs set the ringside price at $100 a pop, an unheard-of sum at that time.

The gate fell short $2 million, far from Jacobs' ballyhooed expectations. After all the hype, only 45,000 fans bought seats for the June 19, 1946, battle, some 10,000 less than Jacobs' prediction. The fight was also an artistic flop. At thirty-two, Louis was now a slow-moving target. Conn, at 182 pounds and four years younger than the champ, was a sad imitation of the prewar fighter. He no longer fought, wrote columnist Jimmy Cannon, with "wise nimbleness." In the eighth round, Conn finally fell victim to a series of blows from Louis. Joe's share of the purse was $591,000, which helped to pay some of his debts. But the bout will be remembered as the beginning of Louis's decline as a great heavyweight.

What I saw at Yankee Stadium is in no record book and has no official standing of any kind. It happened in the second game of a doubleheader between the Yanks and Tigers around 1946 or 1947. It was a dreary day, with on-and-off rain, a terrible day to see one game, no less two. Hank Greenberg hit a ball down the right-field line that seemed to lose itself in its own trajectory as it reached a height above the third tier and then held there, moving slow as the moon across a harvest sky until, beyond expectation, it vanished over the roof and into the Bronx. There seemed to be a second or two, measured only by a hike of uncertainty in the shoulders of the home plate umpire, before the ball was finally called foul. But that fraction of an instant for me was an infinity—and within it I know I saw the only fair ball ever hit out of Yankee Stadium.

**David Falkner,
author of biographies
of Mickey Mantle and
Billy Martin**

Three months later, on September 27, Rocky Graziano, who had come out of the poverty of New York's Lower East Side, fought the first of three brutal battles with Tony Zale of Gary, Indiana. This one took place at the Stadium with 40,000 watching, and it was a crowd pleaser from the opening bell. Neither fighter believed much in defense. Their faces were the best proof of that. Zale kayoed Rocky in six bloody rounds.

"I threw everything at him but the ring posts, my house, and my car," Rocky later said. "The other guy was hurt, bleeding, his mouth was hanging open, and yet I got knocked out for the first time in my life."

The two gladiators fought a second time the next summer in Chicago, and Rocky reversed the verdict, stopping Zale in six hectic rounds, to become middleweight champ. But that first fight was the one that Rocky felt was a disgrace to his manhood.

In 1947, Larry MacPhail dictated the choice of Stanley "Bucky" Harris, who was once the "boy wonder" of the Washington Senators, in 1924–25, as pilot of the Yankees. Harris was known as an affable man, but he hadn't done much winning after leaving the Senators. He took over a team that had added several interesting and potentially productive players. Allie Reynolds, a big right-hander who had a Creek Indian lineage, came over from Cleveland for second-baseman Joe Gordon, in a trade that drew the wrath of many New York fans. But Reynolds quickly emerged as one of the top pitchers of his era, working in both starting roles and relief. Vic Raschi, another pitcher, joined Reynolds on the staff from the Pacific Coast League. They would prevail for years on the mound, giving the Yankees a devastating one-two right-handed punch.

George McQuinn, a bust in 1946 with the A's after a lengthy career with the Browns, was assigned to first base. He didn't make anyone forget Gehrig, but he became a solid performer. The most serendip-

itous addition was a gnomelike lad named Lawrence Peter "Yogi" Berra. By any standards, Yogi might have been the homeliest Yankee since the Babe. To look at him, a squat figure, with a gap between his front teeth and a pitted face, however, brought only smiles of pleasure. For he was a decent, kind fellow, virtues not to be scoffed at in such an ego-driven trade.

And, oh, yes, he also possessed a potent southpaw swing that was custom-made for the right-field Yankee porch. At first, Yogi was used in the outfield, but in time he became a catcher with few peers. When he opened his mouth, Yogi invariably enriched the language with unending pearls of malaprop wisdom. It's possible that Yogi became more famous for his saying "It's déjà vu all over again" and "It's never over till it's over" than for his superb nineteen years as a Yankee. But nobody laughed when this powerful little man dragged his bludgeon to home plate.

On Sunday, April 27, 1947, another watershed moment took place at the Stadium when a debilitated Babe Ruth, suffering from a tumor that affected his larynx, journeyed up from Florida to be present for a day named in his honor. All the other major-league teams joined in the tribute, but the one at the Stadium was the most poignant. Before a packed house, the Babe struggled through a brief, extemporaneous speech, in a hoarse croak that brought tears to the eyes of thousands.

"The only real game, I think, in the world is baseball," said the Babe. "You've got to start from way down, when you're six or seven years old . . . you've got to let it grow up with you, and if you're successful and try hard enough, you're bound to come out on top."

The World Series that year afforded the Yankees the opportunity to compete against the Dodgers' Jackie Robinson, baseball's black pioneer. While other teams had started to add black athletes to their rosters, the Yankees appeared to be stuck in a time warp on this social issue. It would be another half dozen years before they added a black man to their lineup, even though they had a chance to appreciate the talents of Robinson in the '47 Series.

Few previous Series, with or without the Yankees, generated the level of excitement of the '47 games between the archrivals from Brooklyn and New York. The seven-game set, ultimately captured by the Yankees, produced record receipts of over $2 million and was also the first to be televised for $65,000. Two episodes in the Series will forever remain in the all-time memory book.

In the fourth game, Bill Bevens, a thirty-one-year-old journeyman right-hander, was on the verge of hurling the first no-hitter in Series history. He had gone 8⅔ innings without yielding a hit, although his strange performance was somewhat tarnished by the ten walks that he distributed. With the score 2–1 in favor of the Yankees, and Carl Furillo on first with a walk, Al Gionfriddo ran for Furillo and stole second. With first base open, Manager Harris violated conventional baseball wisdom by ordering Bevens to walk pinch-hitter Reiser. That, of course, put the winning run on base, in defiance of the game's logic. Seconds later pinch-hitter Cookie Lavagetto, a veteran infielder sent up to the plate by Manager Burt Shotton, smashed an outside pitch on a line toward the right-field wall. It was too high for Tommy Henrich to catch. Before he could retrieve the bouncing ball, two Brooklyn pinch-runners scampered across the plate with the tying and winning runs. Ebbets Field was a madhouse, Bevens had lost his no-hitter, and the Series was tied at two games each. An ironic footnote to this drama was that Bevens never pitched in a regular-season major-league contest again.

The Yankees tamped down the Brooklyn noise the next day, with a 2–1 victory, sending the Series back to the Stadium for a sixth game. The largest Series crowd in history—74,065—jammed every inch of the ball park and again saw the little-regarded Gionfriddo emerge as an unexpected hero. With the Dodgers in front 8–5 in the sixth inning, the Yankees put runners on first and second, with two out. Up stepped DiMaggio, already possessor of two homers in the Series. He drove a soaring fly off Joe Hatten to the visitors' bull pen, some 415 feet away, in left field. Racing almost blindly to the bull pen, Gionfriddo, only moments before placed in the game as a defensive measure, lurched over the railing and snared the ball. Had it escaped his glove, the ball would have certainly gone in for a game-tying home run.

As Joe approached second base and looked up to see Gionfriddo make his sensational catch, he kicked at the dirt, in an unusual, out-of-character gesture of frustration. When he walked out to his center-field position, Joe was still talking to himself. The Dodgers held on to win that day, sending the Series into a seventh game at the Stadium. But the last game was anti-climactic, as the Yankees won, 5–2, for still another world championship.

As if there hadn't been enough Sturm und Drang at this point, a teary-eyed Larry MacPhail suddenly announced at the post-Series celebration that he was quitting and selling his one-third interest in the club to Topping and Webb. MacPhail's move certainly took

As I walked up the stadium ramp in May 1948, at my first big-league game, with my parents and two sisters, the infield and outfield looked to me like one monstrous carpet of green. It was truly breathtaking. At age nine I was used to playing ball on an asphalt infield, with pebbles and dirt making up the outfield. The Yankees won that day against the A's, but that wasn't important. What *was* important was that I got hooked for life. This is baseball, I thought, I love it!

**Barry Halper,
collector of baseball
memorabilia and a limited
partner of the Yankees**

ABOVE: On June 13, 1948, just two months before he died, Babe Ruth bravely attended ceremonies celebrating Yankee Stadium's twenty-fifth anniversary. Yankee opponents as well as Yankee fans were delighted by the Bambino's appearance. "Nostalgia dripped all over the Yankee Stadium yesterday in the wake of weeping skies," Arthur Daley wrote in *The New York Times*. OPPOSITE: Babe Ruth's battle against cancer ended on August 16, 1948. The flag in front of Yankee Stadium's center-field bleachers was lowered to half-staff the next day. FOLLOWING PAGE: Babe Ruth's casket being carried into Yankee Stadium.

The Babe's Farewell
by Pete Hamill

That August morning in 1948, the newspapers were still full of the story. Babe Ruth was dead. The greatest home run hitter who ever lived had lost his painful battle with cancer. Flags flew at half-mast. Prayers were said in churches and synagogues. At Sanew's candy store in our neighborhood in Brooklyn, my brother Tommy and I bought all seven daily newspapers, plus the *Brooklyn Eagle,* gazing in wonder at the black-bordered photographs of the man they called the Bambino. We cut out the stories, photographs, and cartoons and pasted them with mucilage into a scrapbook. We wanted to save every piece of the event. After all, this was history, and we hadn't witnessed much of it. Or so we thought. Tommy was eleven. I was thirteen.

The year before, we had seen baseball and history joined for the first time, when Jackie Robinson came to play for the Dodgers. With Robinson, we sensed that nothing would ever again be the same, and we were right. But the death of Babe Ruth wasn't about glorious beginnings or grace under pressure; it was the end of a story that was more myth than history, as remote and mysterious to us as the tales of Greek gods we read in the public library.

There was one difference: the body of this immortal would be laid out in the rotunda of Yankee Stadium. Neither Achilles nor Zeus ever said goodbye from the Bronx.

When we read this in the newspaper, we wanted to leave immediately for that distant northern borough. It didn't matter that we had never been there before; in that infinitely more innocent New York, the young lived without a

sense of menace. We hesitated because Babe Ruth was the ultimate Yankee. In Brooklyn, in the years after the war, this was no small thing. As adepts in the secular religion that worshiped in Ebbets Field, we sneered at the Giants and feared the Cardinals, but we hated the Yankees. They were arrogant. They were too perfect. They had beaten us in seven games the previous October in the World Series, in spite of Lavagetto's pinch hit in the ninth inning that broke up Bill Bevens' no-hitter, in spite of Al Gionfriddo's amazing catch of Joe DiMaggio's long drive. Yankee Stadium might have been the House that Ruth Built; to us it was the enemy camp.

So we debated the question with talmudic intensity, and in the end, headed for the subway. After all, Ruth wasn't *always* a Yankee. In the second game of the 1916 World Series, he had pitched for the Boston Red Sox against the Dodgers and lasted 14 great innings before the Red Sox won it, 2–1. If the Dodgers had to lose, at least they lost to Babe Ruth—as a pitcher! And hadn't the Babe, scorned by the Yankees, finished his career as a coach for the Dodgers in 1938? Of course. The papers kept insisting on another big point: Ruth wasn't just a Yankee; he was baseball.

And so, in an example of what Catholic theologians called an "elastic conscience," we took the subway to say a farewell prayer for George Herman Ruth.

Almost a half century later, I don't remember what trains we took, and neither does my brother Tom. But I remember clearly coming around a corner in the Bronx and seeing Yankee Stadium for the first time. It was huge and clean and perfect, like a brand-new Cadillac compared with the rickety model A of Ebbets Field. The day was hot. Vendors filled the streets, selling photographs and souvenirs of the Babe. And as we joined the huge line that hugged the wall of the stadium, we could smell loamy earth, the fresh humid odor of outfield grass.

I tried to imagine what Babe Ruth must have looked like as he moved around on that grass, in the house that he built with his 42-ounce bat. There was no television then, and the newsreels only showed Ruth taking his gigantic swings and sending balls to places where they had never landed before. We never once saw him catch a ball. In all those photographs, we saw a heavy, pigeon-toed man. Surely he couldn't run like Robinson. Certainly he could not chase down a ball as well as Duke Snider, who had come up to the Dodgers in 1946 too. We didn't even think (standing in line, heady with the perfume of a summer ball park, murmuring to each other lest Yankee fans discover our secret National League hearts) he could have fielded the position as well as Terry Moore of the Cardinals.

Still, he was Babe Ruth. And he was dead. So we stopped our own chatter, cut off our doubts, and waited on line among the Irishmen and the Italians, the Jews and the Latinos, the blacks and Germans, the mechanics and the stockbrokers, the waitresses and welders and boys like us. We waited, that is, with the people of New York.

At last, we were a few feet from the coffin. It was open to the summer air. And I remember the silence. It wasn't ordered. It wasn't even demanded. But there was a hush there in the shadows of the rotunda, and the hush made even two boys sense the finality of death. We arrived at the coffin and stared down at the face of the greatest home run hitter on the planet. His eyes were closed and he wore an expression of exhaustion. His skin was loose and powdery.

I whispered a Hail Mary and moved on. We lingered on the sidewalk for only a moment, gazing up at the looming perfect bulk of the stadium. On principle, we did not go inside. We did not look at home plate, or the grass of the outfield. This was not our church. But just before we hurried home to Brooklyn, I was certain I could hear the crack of a bat and a huge deafening roar as Babe Ruth put another brick in the walls of his house.

some of the luster away from the Yankees triumph, although Topping and Webb were hardly inconsolable. When asked why he retired, MacPhail snapped, "Because I wanted to!"

After thirty-three months of MacPhail, things quieted down around the club, as George Weiss, the head of the Yankees' farm system—and a man who exhibited little humor—took over as general manager. With the coming of Weiss, Ed Barrow was out.

By mid-August of 1948, the Babe finally succumbed to cancer, after a long, painful struggle. His last weeks were made relatively peaceful through the constant administration of morphine and other painkilling drugs. But at the end, the once-powerful body was almost unrecognizable. The Babe's home run bashing had, indeed, saved baseball. Then he had made Yankee Stadium known around the world. He would forever symbolize, as a folk hero to beat all folk heroes, the might and brilliance of the Yankees.

In 1948, the Yankees featured DiMaggio, who batted in 155 runs, while their Big Three on the mound—Reynolds, Raschi, and Ed Lopat—won a total of 52 games. The team didn't win the pennant that year, however, suffering elimination on the next-to-last day of the campaign.

Within a year after the Babe was gone, Weiss hired a man destined to become another Yankees icon. After Harris was dismissed as manager, Charles Dillon "Casey" Stengel, already well along in life, at fifty-nine, and carrying the baggage of many failures as a manager in different ports, was unleashed as Weiss's choice to succeed Bucky. When Casey, the Giants and Dodgers warrior of the 1920s, was unveiled as the new manager, many in the New York press couldn't believe it. Wasn't this the same fellow that almost three decades before had scrambled to a home run inside the park in the World Series against the Yankees, causing humorist Will Rogers to chortle, "I never saw a man run faster than that, unless he was running away from the sheriff"?

Stengel, after all, had rightfully won a reputation as a chronic clown and persistent double-talker, whose rambling, elliptical, often slyly caustic phrases had gained a place in the dictionary. Stengelese, it was called. He was able to laugh off defeat in the past by his muddled jokes and his accessibility to the press. But Weiss was shrewd enough to know that Casey was an astute student of the game, with a remarkably retentive memory for just about everything, except the names of players.

Stengel also had learned to handle men, even if he didn't care about winning popularity contests with them. He started each season in spring training by telling his charges to "line up in size place, alphabetically."

Born in Kansas City, Missouri (thus his nickname, joining the K and C to make Casey), Stengel was originally supposed to be a dentist, but he bowed out, according to his story, because people probably wouldn't want to have their teeth worked over by a left-hander.

There probably wasn't a soul in New York who envisioned Casey as the rightful heir to the managerial wisdom of Huggins and McCarthy. Some, perhaps, looked at him as a transitional manager, a fill-in before Weiss could find somebody else. But wouldn't all of these nay-sayers wind up with egg on their faces? In the next twelve years, starting with 1949, he would weave his wand through ten pennants and seven world championships and enough laughs to win him the designation of The Old Professor.

Considering what happened to many of his personnel during that first year, Stengel might have been forgiven for thinking he was back managing the Boston Bees. DiMaggio, with an aching heel, full of painful calcium deposits, missed the first 65 games. Disabling injuries put a number of Yankees into the infirmary at one time or another during the 1949 season, with seven men alternating at first base. Berra was shifted to catcher from the outfield and the shrimp shortstop

Rizzuto became the club's "iron man," because he came to work every day without first reporting to trainer Gus Mauch.

In the face of such nagging medical problems, Casey became an improvising manager, shuffling players in and out of the lineup so fast that he probably forgot from day to day who was playing. Harold Rosenthal, the *Herald-Tribune* writer, was the first to describe what Stengel was doing as "platooning." The term stuck to Casey, just as "push-button pilot" became a permanent disparagement to McCarthy.

Not having played an inning all year, DiMaggio finally got back into the Yankee lineup in late June, when the Yankees were in Boston. The fabulous invalid literally wrecked the Red Sox in a three-game series, as he hit four home runs, batted in nine runs, and fielded everything that came his way. As the Red Sox lost all three games, Casey knew then that the pennant struggle would go down to the wire between his club and Boston as they would meet again in the last two games of the regular season. It did. On the last weekend of the season the Red Sox came into the Stadium holding a one-game lead, with two games to play. They needed only one victory to sew up the flag, the Yankees had to win both.

On Saturday, October 1, with 69,000 true believers howling their support of Casey's wounded warriors at the Stadium, the Yankees won, 5–4, on a home run by Johnny Lindell in the eighth inning. That set the stage for the Sunday game, a winner-take-all proposition that had New York burning with baseball fever. Not even Casey's tortured syntax could begin to describe such a fateful moment. Vic Raschi, facing Red Sox right-hander Ellis Kinder, had the Red Sox down, 1–0, in the last of the eighth inning, when the Yankees broke loose with a crushing four-run rally. Still breathing, the Red Sox retaliated with two in the ninth. But they came up short, sending a crowd of over 68,000 home deliriously happy.

There were many more victories to come for Casey, but this first one was the sweetest of all. Not even the Series victory that followed, in five games over Brooklyn, pleased Casey more than the manner in which his team had risen to the occasion to smite the Red Sox. If there was a mysterious curse on the Red Sox, as not a few mythologists hinted, from the day Boston let the Babe come to New York, the Sox certainly dutifully played out the script.

Late in the next season Mel Allen, the announcer widely popular for his exuberance and incisive reporting, was honored at the Stadium on Mel Allen Day. Over 50,000 fans showered him with gifts and cash. In an act much in keeping with his gentlemanly persona, Allen contributed the money to Columbia University for a Lou Gehrig Scholarship Fund and also for a Babe Ruth Scholarship Fund in Alabama, Mel's native state.

In that year, 1950, Casey's men won again, by three games over Detroit. They followed this triumph with an astonishingly easy destruction of the Phillies in the World Series. A new young pitcher, Edward "Whitey" Ford, as blond as he was cocky, and a native New Yorker to boot, augmented the already superb pitching staff. In the Series the Phillies, affectionately known as the Whiz Kids, accumulated only 26 hits in four straight losses.

Notwithstanding the Yankees' grand home run tradition, the one home run that monopolized the attention of the country's fans in 1951 didn't happen to be hit by a Yankee. It was the work of the New York Giants' Bobby Thomson, who shut the door on Brooklyn with his legendary ninth-inning blast off the stunned Ralph Branca, in the decisive game of the National League playoff. But when Thomson and Durocher's Giants faced the Yankees in the World Series, there were no more miracles for the Polo Grounders. The Yankees beat the Giants, four games to two, to win their third straight Series under the irrepressible Stengel.

Overshadowing the latest Yankee victory was the retirement of DiMaggio, following a .263 season, with just 12 homers. At thirty-seven, Joe found his talents sadly diminished by time and nagging injuries. These grim details dictated that he make a retreat from the game in which he excelled more than any other man, with the possible exception of Ted Williams. The Yankees wanted Joe to stay on, even offering him more money than he'd made at his peak. But he felt it was the moment for him to move on. His timing never had been questioned before, and now, in making this crucial decision about the rest of his life, Joe refused to knuckle under to sentiment.

PREVIOUS PAGES: LONG LINES OF FANS STEPPED SLOWLY INTO THE STADIUM AND PAST THE BABE'S CASKET. OPPOSITE: DURING A PREGAME EXHIBITION ON JUNE 8, 1948, BABE DIDRIKSON ZAHARIAS, A MULTITALENTED ATHLETE, PITCHED TO SEVERAL YANKEE BATTERS IN AN OUTFIT NOT ESPECIALLY SUITED TO THE PURPOSE. ABOVE: YANKEE MANAGER CASEY STENGEL POSING UNCOMFORTABLY WITH JOE DIMAGGIO, JR., FOR A PICTURE TAKEN EARLY IN 1949. JOE SR. WAS OUT WITH A HEEL SPUR INJURY AT THE TIME, AND STENGEL, IN HIS FIRST YEAR AS YANKEE MANAGER, WAS HAVING SOME DIFFICULTY GETTING ALONG WITH THE YANKEE CLIPPER.

Following the Yankees' last-game victory over the Red Sox that delivered the 1949 pennant, Casey Stengel registers an expression of weary pride in the clubhouse. Celebrating with him are Yogi Berra (on the left) and Hank Bauer.

Waiting in the wings for DiMaggio's departure was a kid, barely past nineteen, who had been signed to a contract in 1949, for a bonus of $1,000. Soon he would dominate the hopes and dreams of a new generation of Yankees aficionados. Mickey Charles Mantle, born in Spavinaw, Oklahoma, came to play at 200 pounds and 6 feet. He had muscles that bulged like pontoons and his legs appeared as rugged as mighty oaks. He was fair and blue-eyed and "his face was as open as the part of America he came from," wrote Leonard Shecter. His father, Mutt, was a baseball nut who had named his son after Gordon S. "Mickey" Cochrane, a spirited catcher for the Athletics in the 1930s. Mutt also had taught Mickey from the start to hit from both sides of the plate.

In no time at all Mickey was hailed as the successor to DiMaggio, even before he had cracked a single hit in the Stadium. "When he hits the ball," said his admirers, "it even sounds different." At least, it was insisted, he was as good as that new Giants star, Willie Mays, whose effervescence and talent were now on display at the Polo Grounds.

That first year, there was a hitch in midsummer, when Mickey was sent back to Kansas City for a decompression session in the minors. But he returned to the Yankees not long after, to play right field. In the World Series against the Giants, DiMaggio was in center field, while Mickey played in right. And it was in that Series that Mickey stepped in a Stadium drain cover while chasing a ball in right-center. His right knee was sprained badly enough for him to miss the rest of the Series. But it was also the first of a succession of leg injuries that damaged his body, if not his spirit.

While the Yankees watched Mickey's ups and downs, in 1951 another Oklahoman, Allie Reynolds, put the ugly rumors about his heart and guts to rest. Within a space of ten weeks, Reynolds delivered two no-hitters. The first came against Cleveland in July,

Thank the Good Lord for making me a Yankee. . . . I suppose we get more sentimental as we get older. That day they had for me, more than any at Yankee Stadium, gave me an awful lot of satisfaction-a feeling that I'd done a pretty good job with the only talent I had.

Joe DiMaggio, in 1949, after receiving a speedboat, a TV set, a radio, watches, a Cadillac, jewelry, a bicycle for his little son Joe, and an automobile for his mother, at Joe DiMaggio Day at Yankee Stadium

the second in September against the Red Sox, before 40,000 at the Stadium on a picture postcard Indian summer day. Until that time, only Johnny Vander Meer of Cincinnati had ever tossed two no-hitters in one season. Johnny did it back to back, however, in 1938, a feat that has never been duplicated.

Reynolds' second no-hit achievement was especially noteworthy, because he accomplished it without full cooperation from his catcher, Yogi Berra. With two out in the top of the ninth inning, all that Allie had to do was to retire Ted Williams to complete his second no-hitter. The crowd thrilled to the drama. Imagine having *only* Williams to contend with in such a situation!

Ted watched the first pitch go by for a strike. On the second pitch, Williams swooshed around violently but could produce only a towering foul pop behind home plate. It looked like an easy out for Yogi, who appeared to have it in sight all the way. But as he camped under the ball, Yogi permitted it to bounce off the end of his mitt. As the ball clunked harmlessly to the ground, Reynolds, rushing in to lend moral support, almost tripped over Yogi. The crowd emitted a vast groan, which didn't add to the heartsick Yogi's well-being. "Don't worry, Yogi, we'll get him again," Reyn-

olds quickly advised his catcher.

On the next pitch, another fast ball across the letters, Williams again raised a high, twisting foul behind the plate. It is widely thought that there are no second acts in American life, but this time Yogi surrounded the ball, then gripped it firmly, giving the relieved Reynolds his second no-hitter.

As was the case so often with Yogi, there was an amusing follow-up to the incident. During the off-season, Berra worked in a store as a clothing salesman. One day a father brought his son in to buy a suit. The little boy stared at Yogi for a moment, then inquired how come he dropped the last out of Reynolds' no-hitter. "For a moment

There's the bigness of it. There are those high stands and all the people smoking–and, of course, the shadows. It takes at least one series to get accustomed to the stadium and even then you're not sure.

**Ted Williams,
in *Life* magazine, shortly
after his retirement, in 1960**

I felt like crowning the kid and I gave him a terrible look," recalled Yogi. "Then I remembered, the customer's always right, so I told him he had nothing to worry about. If you want, I said, I'll autograph both sleeves of the suit for you."

In the 1950s, the Stadium, which could be rented by almost anybody, became a gathering place for the Jehovah's Witnesses, a proselytizing Christian sect. The Witnesses came from all over the world, for a program lasting eight days. They even brought their own folding chairs with them. They filled the Stadium with enormous crowds, up to 120,000, and were singularly well behaved, perhaps more so than the average baseball crowd. They did their own housekeeping afterward, sweeping the entire Stadium and scrubbing down every seat with soap and water. Four hundred brooms were supplied to the Witnesses, and every broom was returned. When the Witnesses insisted on

There was a great, dark mystery about it when I first came here from Oklahoma. I still get goose pimples just walking inside it. Now I think this is about the prettiest ball park I ever saw.
Mickey Mantle, 1976

using the playing field, as well as the stands, they were informed that wasn't permitted because the turf would be torn up. So a compromise was reached: they all took off their shoes.

In what was a veritable miracle of preparation and logistics, the Yankees were able to play on a Sunday

OPPOSITE: DOZENS OF OPPONENTS HAVE PLAYED SUPERBLY IN YANKEE STADIUM, NONE MORE SO THAN TED WILLIAMS OF THE BOSTON RED SOX. SEEN HERE DURING BATTING PRACTICE IN 1949, WILLIAMS NEARLY LED HIS TEAM TO A PENNANT WIN. HE HIT .343, WITH 159 RBIS AND FORTY-THREE HOME RUNS THAT SEASON. ABOVE: LOOK CLOSELY BETWEEN "STRIKES" AND "BALLS" AND YOU'LL SEE THE YANKEE STADIUM SCOREBOARD OPERATOR PEERING THROUGH A SMALL OPENING AS THE FIRST GAME OF THE 1949 WORLD SERIES BEGINS. FOLLOWING PAGES: IT WAS GENERALLY ACCEPTED THAT MOST YANKEE SUBSTITUTES WOULD HAVE BEEN STARTERS FOR OTHER TEAMS DURING THE FORTIES AND FIFTIES. OUTFIELDERS IN 1949 INCLUDED (FROM THE LEFT) GENE WOODLING, HANK BAUER, CLIFF MAPES, JOHNNY LINDELL, JOE DIMAGGIO, AND CHARLEY KELLER.

Milestones and Happenings

1925–46: Notre Dame vs. Army football rivalry.

1920s–1930s: Fordham vs. Pittsburgh football games.

November 11, 1928: Notre Dame defeats Army, after Coach Knute Rockne delivers his legendary "Win One for the Gipper" speech in the locker room.

1920s–1930s: NYU football games.

1929: Yankees are the first team to wear numbers on the backs of their uniforms.

May 30, 1938: 81,841 paid, a Stadium record, to see a Memorial Day doubleheader against Boston.

May 28, 1946: Yankees play first night game, lose to Washington Senators.

1956–73: New York Giants football games.

December 28, 1958: Baltimore Colts defeat Giants, 23–17, in overtime to win NFL title. Game is called "greatest ever played."

1968–87: Grambling football games.

1960s–1970s: Soccer games, featuring Pele.

1950s: Circus and rodeo.

1950s: Jehovah's Witnesses pack Stadium.

July 20, 1957: The Reverend Billy Graham preaches.

December 12, 1957: Cardinal Spellman celebrates Mass.

October 4, 1965: Pope Paul VI visits Stadium on first papal trip to North America.

April 9, 1968: Poet Marianne Moore throws out the first ball.

October 2, 1969: Pope John Paul II appears in second papal visit.

October 7, 1979: Pope John Paul II appears in third papal visit.

May 1, 1986: Cardinal O'Connor officiates at Youth World Assembly Day.

June 21, 1990: South Africa's Nelson Mandela is welcomed.

June 22, 1990: Billy Joel performs.

August 29, 1992: U2 performs.

June 10, 1994: Pink Floyd performs.

---

afternoon at the Stadium, even if the Witnesses were scheduled to assemble the next morning at nine. Tents, trucks, food, loudspeakers sprang up almost out of nowhere, as Yankee officials couldn't help but marvel at such quick efficiency.

Billy Graham, the world-famous preacher, realized that his own form of arena evangelism was also perfectly suited for Yankee Stadium. Before exuberant Stadium crowds, he thundered his revival-meeting message, leading the way for others to utilize the ball park for nonsporting events.

Over the years, the Stadium welcomed Holy Name conclaves, rodeos full of animals, circuses full of clowns, Israel rallies, Youth World Assemblies, celebrations of Mass by Cardinal Spellman, papal visits, and Unification Church meetings. Indeed, the Stadium became the most eclectic ball park in the world, a meeting arena for the secular and the religious and the political. Originally meant as a home for athletic heroes, it became known universally for its hospitality to one and all, even to those who didn't know a baseball glove from a boxing glove.

In the summer of 1952, as Mantle began to rocket his tape measure home runs in his first full season, and Billy Martin, Casey's favorite night-prowling bad boy, was ensconced at second base, the Yankees galloped to their fourth straight American League flag. That June,

OPPOSITE: DURING A VACATION IN NEW YORK SHORTLY AFTER PASSING HIS ALABAMA BAR EXAM IN 1936, MELVIN ALLEN ISRAEL WAS INTERVIEWED BY TED HUSING OF CBS AND ACCEPTED A JOB AS SPORTS AND SPECIAL EVENTS ANNOUNCER. HE BECAME LEAD ANNOUNCER FOR THE YANKEES AND GIANTS IN 1940, WENT INTO THE ARMY IN 1942, AND IN 1946 BEGAN AN EXCLUSIVE ASSIGNMENT WITH THE YANKEES. MEL ALLEN WAS THE YANKEES' VOICE FOR THE NEXT NINETEEN YEARS.

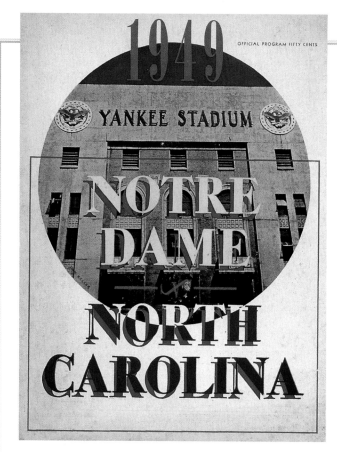

ABOVE: YANKEE STADIUM LOOMED IMPRESSIVELY ON THE
COVER OF THE NOTRE DAME–NORTH CAROLINA PROGRAM
COVER. NOTRE DAME'S PLAYERS INCLUDED LEON HART AND
EMIL "SIX YARD" SITKO, AND NORTH CAROLINA COUNTERED
WITH THE TALENTS OF CHARLIE "CHOO CHOO" JUSTICE.
OPPOSITE: PEANUTS WERE JUST TEN CENTS A BAG DURING
THE EARLY 1950s.

as the Yankees built their lead over Cleveland—mainly
due to the pitching of Reynolds, Raschi, Lopat, and
Johnny Sain—an extraordinary boxing bout took place
at the Stadium. It may rate, as writer W. C. Heinz has
said, as "the most bizarre championship fight of our
time." Few would disagree with him.

Middleweight champ Sugar Ray Robinson, enshrined under the cliché that he was "pound for pound
the best fighter in the world," got into the ring that
sweltering June 25 night against the light-heavy-
weight champ, Joey Maxim. In his bid to add another
world title to his belt, Sugar Ray gave away 15
pounds to Maxim.

Until the fourteenth round, Sugar Ray won almost every round decisively, as he outpunched, out-
pounded, and outchased the plodding Maxim. In the
process, however, Sugar Ray worked himself into a

state of almost total exhaustion. At ringside that
night, on the hottest June 25 in New York history, it
was 104 degrees. As the bell sounded for the 14th
round, Robinson was "Melted Sugar," for he couldn't
have thrown one more punch or pursued Maxim for
another second. He sat, catatonic in his corner, a victim of his own nonstop aggression.

Earlier, at the end of the tenth round, Referee
Ruby Goldstein suffered a knockout, too. Moving
around the ring after the two fighters, like a sluggish
bug on a hot stove, Goldstein was on the verge of col-
lapse. He had to be removed from the scene and was
replaced by Ray Miller. In the entire history of the
sport, there had never been a substitute referee in-
serted in the middle of a bout. Over 47,000 in the
Stadium, close to drowning in their own sweat, sat
through this agonizing spectacle.

If Sugar Ray had been able to stand on his feet at
the end, he would have had a third world title. But it
wasn't to be. Under the shower, after the battle, the
dazed Sugar Ray could only mutter, "God willed it."

In the World Series against Brooklyn that fall, the
Yankee dynasty continued through a hard-fought
seven-game set. But as the Yankees won the world
crown for the fourth straight time, to match the
1936–39 mark of the Bronx Bombers, the triumph did
not come without a measure of heart fibrillation. In the
seventh inning of the decisive game, as the Yankees
led, 4–2, at Ebbets Field, the Dodgers loaded the bases
with two out.

Jackie Robinson then raised a tantalizing pop fly
close to the mound, as the runners skittered madly
around the bases. At the last moment, Billy Martin,
seeing that nobody else went for the ball, raced in from
second base to grab it, just before it hit the earth. Martin's take-charge lunge, with his cap flying, saved the
game and Series for New York. It also further endeared
the bellicose little man to Stengel.

With the Yankees in the Series again in 1953, it was

Martin redux, leading the Yankees to their fifth Series championship in a row, an all-time mark. At sixty-three years of age, Stengel had progressed from managerial clown in Boston (when he was hit by an automobile some ironic newspaper pundits insisted it was a long-overdue suicide attempt) to unreconstructed genius in New York.

Martin won the Series and the final game at the Stadium against the recidivist Dodgers, with a ninth-inning single. That put the finishing touch on a personal Series rampage—12 hits, including 2 home runs, 2 triples, a double, 7 singles, 8 RBIs—that placed Billy in the same class as such Series one-man shows as the Babe, Christy Mathewson, Gehrig, and Pepper Martin.

Then a funny thing happened on the way to a sixth consecutive pennant and world title. Stengel led another fine team that won 103 games. But it simply wasn't good enough to finish in front of a hot Cleveland club, managed by Al Lopez, that had won 111 games, one more than the previous record set by the 1927 Yankees. The Yankees continued to have great pitching—with Ford, Lopat, Reynolds, and a 20-game-winning Bob Grim

I grew up loving Southern League baseball. When I was four my daddy took me to the old Rickwood Field in Birmingham. Then, coming to Yankee Stadium in 1937 for the first time—where the greats like the Babe, Lou, and DiMag played—was just beyond my dreams. Suddenly, here I was, a guy supposed to practice law, broadcasting Yankee home games on radio from this mecca of baseball. This was *the* place, the number-one place in baseball. The stadium was like the Empire State Building or The Grand Canyon of baseball, and every time I stepped inside of it I had to pinch myself!

**Mel Allen,
for years the Voice of
the Yankees**

on hand—but Lopez superintended a mound corps of astounding abilities. Even the great fireballer Bob Feller was overshadowed on such a staff. Bob Lemon, a converted infielder, won 23, and so did Early Wynn. Mike Garcia snagged 19, and Art Houtteman won 15.

So it was Cleveland that went to the World Series in 1954 against the Giants of Durocher, Mays, and an inspired pinch-hitter named James Lamar "Dusty" Rhodes. When the Indians, heavily favored, proceeded to lose four in a row to the Giants, some wise men insisted the Yankees would have won.

No matter. The Yankees fully appreciated that they needed some new blood to help out Mantle, Berra, and Ford. So they added Moose Skowron to their cast at first base, probably the hardest hitter at that post since Gehrig, and put Tommy Byrne, a slickster of a southpaw, into their mound rotation. But the most radical change occurred when Elston Howard, a poised, talented athlete who could play outfield and catcher, joined the team. He was the first black man to

ABOVE TOP: YANKEE STADIUM IN THE EARLY 1950S; THE BRONX HAS CROWDED AROUND IT, AND THE POLO GROUNDS, ACROSS THE HARLEM RIVER, IS JUST A SUBWAY RIDE AWAY. ABOVE BOTTOM: IN 1950 *THE BOSTON GLOBE* PUBLISHED A SERIES OF BALL PARK PROFILES, WRITTEN AND ILLUSTRATED BY GENE MACK, REPORTEDLY A DISTANT RELATIVE OF THE PHILADELPHIA ATHLETICS' PATRIARCH CONNIE MACK. GENE MACK'S DRAWINGS RECORDED GREAT PLAYERS AND GREAT EVENTS WITH ACCURATE AND FOND DETAIL.

ABOVE: IN THE FINAL DAYS OF THE 1951 PENNANT RACE, ALLIE REYNOLDS PITCHED A NO-HITTER AGAINST THE RED SOX THAT WAS NEARLY UNDONE WHEN YOGI BERRA DROPPED A POP-UP WITH TWO OUTS IN THE NINTH INNING. YOGI REDEEMED HIMSELF ONE PITCH LATER.

play for the Yankees, who had stood by intransigently for years, as other clubs integrated their rosters. The Yankees always offered an excuse: they were winning without black men. But it was a lame apologia in an era when black players were beginning to dominate major-league play. Stengel, a man from another baseball time, noted at once that Howard, so able in many areas of the game, was not quick afoot. "Well, when they finally get me a nigger," Stengel said, employing language that was not unusual for the dugout, "they get me one who can't run." Those who knew Casey intimately rejected the notion that he was a bigot. They apologized for him, suggesting that he had played early in his career against many blacks, including the wondrous Satchel Paige. They also pointed to the fact that he always treated Elston properly and with regard.

With their new additions, the Yankees climbed back to the top in 1955. And as seemed inevitable, it was the Dodgers who faced them again in the Series. Favored to beat the Brooklyns, the Yankees made it

seem easy, winning the first two games at the Stadium. Then the ceiling suddenly fell in for the Yanks at Ebbets Field, as the Dodgers took three straight in their band-box park. Heading back to the Stadium, the Dodgers felt they had finally found the recipe of success against their New York foes.

Ford tied the Series with a victory in game six, however, sending the classic to game seven at the Stadium. With 63,000 on hand at the Stadium on a gorgeous October Tuesday, twenty-three-year-old Johnny Podres, a southpaw from Witherbee, New York, pitched the

People from out of town say there are three things in New York they want to see—the Statue of Liberty, Radio City, and Yankee Stadium. I guess you could say the stadium is hallowed ground.

Bill Waite,
an employee at the stadium
for over fifty years

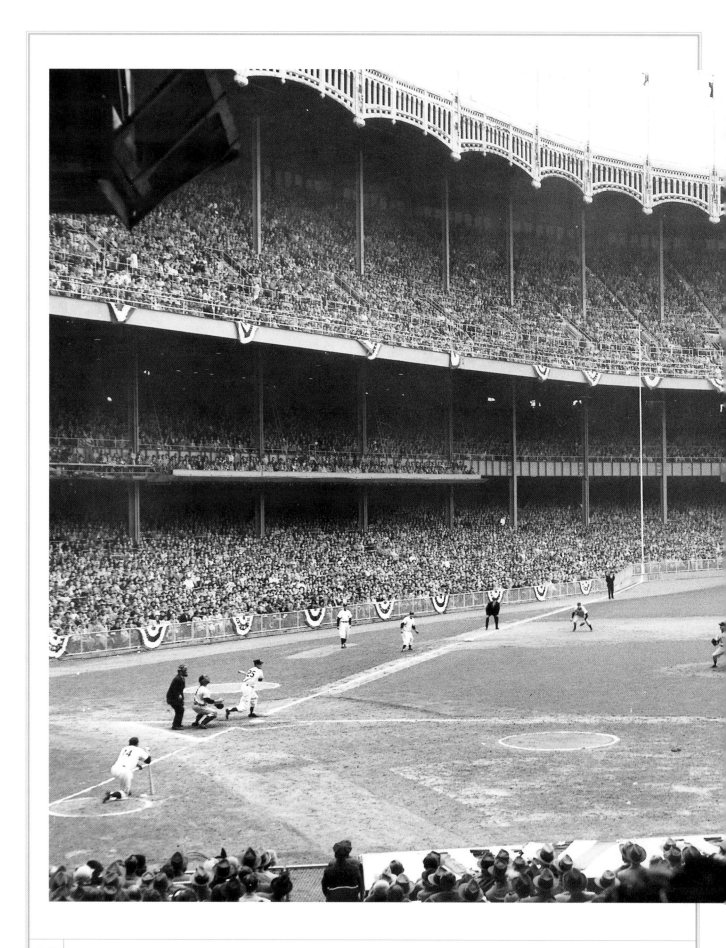

PREVIOUS PAGES: THE YANKEES WON THE 1951 WORLD SERIES FROM THE GIANTS IN SIX GAMES. THE ACTION HERE SHOWS
HANK BAUER TRIPLING WITH THE BASES LOADED IN THE SIXTH INNING OF GAME SIX, PROVIDING A 4–1 YANKEE LEAD. ABOVE: IN
THE SECOND GAME OF THE 1951 WORLD SERIES, MICKEY MANTLE, WHILE AVOIDING A COLLISION WITH JOE DIMAGGIO, STEPPED
ON A DRAIN COVER AND SPRAINED HIS RIGHT KNEE. HE DID NOT PLAY AGAIN IN THE SERIES THAT YEAR, AND WAS AFFLICTED
WITH KNEE AND LEG INJURIES FOR THE REST OF HIS CAREER. OPPOSITE TOP: STANDING ROOM ONLY FOR THE FOURTH GAME OF
THE 1952 WORLD SERIES. THE SCOREBOARD RECORDS PEE WEE REESE AT BAT FOR BROOKLYN IN THE FIRST INNING, FACING
ALLIE REYNOLDS, WHO GAVE UP FOUR SINGLES IN A 2–0 WIN. DEDICATED READERS WILL BE ABLE TO IDENTIFY EVERY OTHER
PLAYER IN THE STARTING LINEUPS. OPPOSITE BOTTOM: JOHNNY MIZE TORMENTED THE DODGERS FOR ELEVEN YEARS WHILE
PLAYING FOR THE CARDINALS AND GIANTS IN THE NATIONAL LEAGUE, THEN WAS DEALT TO THE YANKEES IN 1949. HE IS SEEN
HERE AFTER CLUBBING A THREE-RUN HOMER AGAINST THE DODGERS IN THE FIFTH GAME OF THE 1952 WORLD SERIES. IT WAS
HIS THIRD HOMER OF THE SERIES. YOGI BERRA AND GIL MCDOUGALD ARE OFFERING HANDSHAKES, AND PHIL RIZZUTO IS WAITING
TO DO THE SAME.

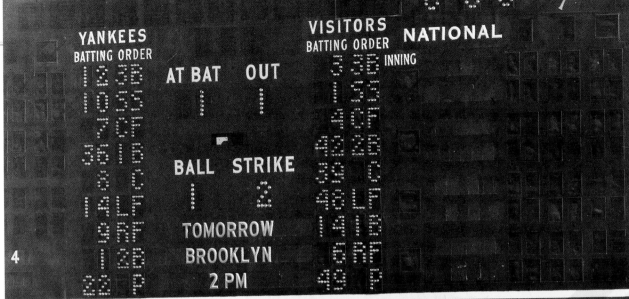

ABOVE: THE NIGHT BEFORE THE FIRST GAME OF THE 1953 WORLD SERIES, CHARLES KIERST OF AUBURN, NEW YORK (ON THE LEFT), AND RALPH BELCORE OF CHICAGO STAKE OUT THEIR PLACES IN LINE FOR BLEACHER TICKETS. THIS WAS THE FIFTH TIME THEY HAD REPEATED THE CEREMONY. FOLLOWING PAGES: THIS SWEEPING VIEW OF YANKEE STADIUM WAS TAKEN BEFORE A PRESEASON GAME BETWEEN THE YANKEES AND BROOKLYN DODGERS IN 1954.

Dodgers to their first World Series victory in history. At long last, the drought against the Yankees had come to an end. The Boys of Summer—including Robinson, PeeWee Reese, Duke Snider, Roy Campanella, Carl Erskine, and Carl Furillo—were fortunate that Podres never pitched a better game. But there was a bit of strategy that also worked out for the Dodgers.

In the sixth inning, Junior Gilliam was shifted to second base, from left field, with Sandy Amoros, an unheralded little fellow from Havana, taking over left field. The first two Yankees then got on base. With nobody out and Podres nursing a 2–0 margin, the left-handed Berra sliced a long, opposite-field drive down the left-field foul line. Having been pulled toward center field, Amoros didn't look as if he could race to the ball some 100 feet away and make the catch. But he did, right in front of the stand. Today "the catch" is almost as much honored as Mays' sensational grab in the '54 Series.

Even more important to the outcome of the game and Series, however, was the throw that Amoros unleashed to double up the runner on first. It broke the back of the Yankee rally. Podres then went on to complete his shutout, as Brooklyn fans were beside themselves with joy. Their euphoria was well earned and long overdue. "Next year" had at last arrived for them.

Of all the Yankees, only Rizzuto, at shortshop, and coaches Bill Dickey and Frank Crosetti had ever experienced a World Series loss. That was in 1942, when the Cardinals overcame the Yanks, before so many players marched off to war.

But the merciless Yankees, specialists in being killjoys, didn't take long to get back on the winning track. The very next year, the two teams were at it again in the Series. This time the Yankees wouldn't be caught short by fate or substitution. For they owned a big pitcher, Donald James Larsen, who was ready to use all the might and skill in his 235 pounds and 6'4" frame to frustrate the Brooklyn team.

In November 1954, the Yankees completed an eighteen-player trade with Baltimore that brought Larsen to New York, after he'd experienced a disastrous 3–21 season with the Orioles. Larsen's good fortune in coming to New York was not at first matched by his good sense, for his bibulous conduct was hardly more exemplary than that of such legendary boulevardiers as Flint Rhem, Rube Waddell, and Bugs Raymond. In short, he was a blithe spirit, a midnight crawler, whom the writers euphemistically described as "fun-loving."

Stengel had reasonable success handling the right-hander, even though Larsen challenged a telephone pole with his convertible one early Florida morning during spring training of 1956. Indeed, Larsen was picked to open the season by Stengel and came through with a victory over Washington, just to prove that Casey's forbearance was the proper medicine. By the end of the '56 season, Don had amassed an 11–5 mark, including four straight wins in the final month. This surprising second wind helped to install the Yankees in the World Series against Brooklyn.

In the second Series game, Don handed out passes like a crazed press agent. He was under a hot shower and on top of a cold beer before two innings were completed. "That's the last time I go to bed early," commented Don.

Notwithstanding this mediocre performance, Casey brought Larsen back for the fifth game, when the Series was knotted at two games each. When Casey informed Don that he'd be pitching the fifth game, Larsen prepared for the event by visiting one of his favorite Manhattan haunts, accompanied by a sportswriter, Art Richman, who had befriended Don from the moment he'd set foot in New York. Around midnight, the two hopped a cab for the return trip to the Bronx. Don downed a pizza pie in his room at the Concourse Plaza Hotel, perused the Sunday comics, his favorite reading matter, then remarked to Richman that he hadn't gone to church that morning. To atone for this omission, Don pulled out a twenty-dollar bill and handed it to Richman with the suggestion that he give it to his favorite church.

"I don't go to church," Richman reminded him. "I go to synagogue."

OFFICIAL TIME
LONGINES
World's Most Honored Watch

ZENITH   RADIOS   ...IP MORRIS

TELEVISION

1 2 3 4 5 6 7 8 9 10   R H E

BROOKLYN
YANKEES   Yankees

AMERICAN   YANKEES   VISITORS   NATIONAL
INNING   BATTING ORDER   BATTING ORDER   INNING

                        AT BAT   OUT

                        BALL   STRIKE

Disosway & Fisher Inc.

...ONE INTERFERING   UMPIRES — PLATE 3   OPENING DAY
WITH PLAY   BASES 2-4-1   THURS. APRIL 15
...BJECT TO ARREST   PHILA 2 PM

STADIUM   GE
FAVORITE BALLANTINE 🥨 ALE
                          BEER   BLADE

EXIT   EXIT

                        407 FT.

                                                           BKLYN.
                                                           YANKS

"Then tell your mom to give it to your synagogue," replied Larsen.

When Don awoke on Monday morning at eight, he joined the long line of Series pitchers who had had to do combat with stomach butterflies. "I thought I'd never get to sleep," he mumbled. When he got to the ball park, he still felt fidgety.

As the day went on, however, and as 64,000 watched at the Stadium, Don proceeded to set down Dodger batters one inning after another. His rival on the mound, Sal Maglie, gave him stiff competition, but that afternoon Larsen simply couldn't be beaten or surpassed. With his newly acquired no-windup delivery, Larsen entered the seventh inning with a 2–0 lead over one of the most devastating baseball lineups of the century. More than that, he hadn't permitted a single enemy player to reach base.

In the second inning, Robinson banged a line drive off third-baseman Andy Carey's glove, but shortstop Gil McDougald retrieved the ball and threw to first for the out. In the fifth inning, Mantle robbed Gil Hodges with a splendid backhand catch in center field. That was as close as any Brooklyn player got to reaching base safely.

By the eighth inning, the crowd was on its feet, roaring with each pitch. But this was one day when Larsen was not to be denied. With two out in the ninth, Dale Mitchell, a pinch-hitter, took a called third strike (though many, including Mitchell, thought it was a foot outside the plate). Larsen had his perfecto—the first in Series history, the first perfect game in the big leagues since 1922, and to this day the only game of its kind ever pitched in the World Series. Vin Scully, the Brooklyn announcer, proclaimed that "it most assuredly was the greatest game ever pitched in the history of baseball." And the facts tended to reinforce his judgment: 97 pitches thrown, 71 strikes, 26 balls, no hits, no walks, no hit batsmen, no errors, no runs. In short, absolutely nothing.

In his postmortem, the flabbergasted Larsen acknowledged he'd had "a couple" before the game. So it stood to reason, he added, "that I'm gonna have a couple the night after."

My two brothers and I used a Little League bat and a badminton shuttlecock and we laid out a baseball field in miniature to the exact proportions of Yankee Stadium, very short right field, very deep center. . . . We took all our lamps out of the living room for night games and put them on extension cords, spreading them around the field with no shades on, so they gave off a good Yankee Stadium glow. . . . The first game I went to at Yankee Stadium, in 1956, I sat in Louis Armstrong's seats (my family was in the music business), and Mickey signed my scorecard and hit a home run. From then on, when I went to the stadium I thought Mickey knew I was there and was telling himself, "Billy's here, I'd better have a good day, I'd better try to hit one for him."

Billy Crystal,
in *Absolutely Mahvelous*

Larsen's perfection was followed by Clem Labine's 1–0 victory over the Yankees, in eleven innings, at Ebbets Field. But the seventh game was almost anticlimactic, with the Yankees winning a 9–0 laugher, as Berra whacked two homers. The Yankees were world champs for the seventeenth time, much to the chagrin of the disappointed and frustrated Brooklyn fans. Equally relevant was the fact that it was the final "subway series" between the Dodgers and the Yankees, because not long after, the Dodgers and Giants heeded the siren call of the golden West and moved to California. The 1956 Series also marked Jackie Robinson's adieu to baseball.

The Yankees were in the Series again the next year, minus Billy Martin, who had been traded in the off-season, presumably because of his well-publicized role in a nightclub incident. Casey wanted his rebel to remain, but he was overruled by the front office. So Martin never had the chance to play in the 1957 Series against Milwaukee. Dominating the Yankees in a way they had never been dominated before, Lew Burdette, a right-handed pitcher often rumored to throw an illegal spitball, defeated the New Yorkers three times in a week's work. Two of Burdette's victories were shutouts, one thrown in Milwaukee and the second one at the Stadium, giving the Braves the world championship. Not since Stan Coveleski of Cleveland trimmed the Dodgers in three complete games in 1920 had anyone equaled the feat. Now Burdette had done it.

The same two clubs won pennants again in 1958, but Burdette failed to duplicate his achievement. Stengel's men rallied from a 3–1 deficit in games to take the Series. Hank Bauer, acting like Babe Ruth, hit four home runs for the Yanks, as the club hung up another world title in seven games.

Following the end of the baseball season, pro football took over Yankee Stadium. The Giants, the reigning power in the East, had been using the premises since 1956. On December 28, 1958, they met the Baltimore Colts for the National Football League crown before 65,000 bundled-up, slightly hysterical fans. A week before the game, Commissioner Bert Bell of the

No-Hitters at Yankee Stadium

August 27, 1938: Monte Pearson, 13–0, vs. Cleveland
April 30, 1946: Bob Feller, Cleveland, 1–0, vs. Yankees
September 28, 1951: Allie Reynolds, 8–0, vs. Boston
August 25, 1952: Virgil Trucks, Detroit, 1–0, vs. Yankees
October 8, 1956: Don Larsen, 2–0, vs. Brooklyn, World Series
July 4, 1983: Dave Righetti, 4–0, vs. Boston
September 4, 1993: Jim Abbott, 4–0, vs. Cleveland
May 14, 1996: Dwight Gooden, 2–0, vs. Seattle

ABOVE: DON LARSEN HAS JUST COMPLETED WHAT IS STILL AN UNMATCHED WORLD SERIES FEAT: A PERFECT GAME. HE ACCOMPLISHED IT IN THE FIFTH GAME OF THE 1956 MATCH WITH THE DODGERS. GIL MCDOUGALD AND YOGI BERRA ARE SEEN FLANKING LARSEN. FOLLOWING PAGES: ON AUGUST 30, 1953, THE YANKEES HELD THEIR ANNUAL OLD-TIMERS GAME. IN THE FRONT ROW (FROM THE LEFT) ARE BILL DICKEY, RED ROLFE, WALLY PIPP, JOE DIMAGGIO, FRANK CROSETTI, PHIL RIZZUTO, EARLE COMBS, BOB SHAWKEY, RED RUFFING, AND LEFTY GOMEZ. STANDING (FROM THE LEFT) ARE WHITEY WITT, ROGER PECKINPAUGH, WAITE HOYT, WALLY SCHANG, LYN LARY, JOE DUGAN, BUDDY HASSETT, WILCEY MOORE, TOMMY HENRICH, JOE GORDON, CHARLEY KELLER, AND HOME RUN BAKER.

ABOVE: MICKEY MANTLE BATTING AGAINST THE KANSAS CITY ATHLETICS ON JUNE 6, 1956. THIS WAS MICKEY'S DEFINING
SEASON, A YEAR IN WHICH HIS .353 AVERAGE, 52 HOMERS, AND 130 RBIS EARNED HIM THE TRIPLE CROWN. OPPOSITE TOP
LEFT: A REGULAR PREGAME RITUAL FOR MICKEY MANTLE THROUGHOUT MOST OF HIS CAREER WAS THE TAPING OF HIS LEGS.
THIS PICTURE, TAKEN EARLY IN HIS CAREER, SHOWS HIM TAPING ONLY HIS RIGHT LEG, INJURED IN THE 1951 WORLD SERIES.
OPPOSITE RIGHT: IN THE FIRST GAME OF THE 1955 WORLD SERIES JACKIE ROBINSON OF THE DODGERS STOLE HOME. THE
"SAFE" CALL BY PLATE UMPIRE BILL SUMMERS SENDS YANKEE CATCHER YOGI BERRA INTO A FIT OF PROTEST.

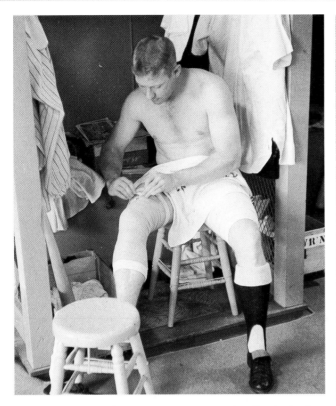

NFL ruled that if the two teams were deadlocked after four quarters, they would continue play until one team scored. Bell didn't anticipate that his decree would be necessary. But as matters developed, the game turned out to be the first to be fought out till "sudden death."

The pro grid game certainly wasn't invented on that chilly afternoon at the Stadium, but it did take a giant leap forward. It was the first step on the way to becoming America's most lionized sport—and, ironi-

Yankee Stadium is something else, a law unto itself. It has earned the right to look any way it pleases and I wouldn't change a seat of it. . . . It is particularly dreamworthy because not so long ago the World Series used to turn up there as regularly as Wimble· don. I once sneaked out to center field myself as a youth to see how things looked from Mickey Man· tle's point of view and felt the same tingle some people get from Civil War battlefields.

Wilfrid Sheed,
in *Baseball and Lesser Sports*

cally, the gestation process had occurred in baseball's own mecca. The reason was simple: The game turned into a clash of such desire and excitement that at its conclusion it was immediately dubbed the ultimate "cardiac contest."

More important, perhaps, was that as a televised spectacle it aroused highly suggestible Madison Avenue and its advertisers. Soon these advertisers would fight to pay their money to get on screen

during the football season. Actually, the game was rather dull for the first half, at which time the Colts led, 14–3. Then the Giants rallied, behind quarterback Charlie Conerly, to take the lead, 17–14, going into the fourth quarter. No sooner had the Giants moved ahead than the Colts, with the help of their passer, Johnny Unitas, firing to his sure-fingered, nearsighted receiver, Raymond Berry, moved down the field. "He catches passes the way most of us catch the common cold," wrote Red Smith about Berry, in a phrase that he borrowed from W. C. Heinz.

With seven seconds to go, the Colts' Steve Myhra kicked a field goal to tie the score at 17-all, sending the game into overtime. A coin was flipped to determine who would receive, and the Giants won. They couldn't make progress toward the Colts' goal line, however, and were forced to punt to the Baltimore 20-yard line. From that point, Unitas sparked a march to victory, with a mix of running and passing plays that culminated, after eight minutes of struggle, in a touchdown by Alan Ameche. As Ameche crashed through to score from the one-yard line, the huge crowd roared, some in agony, others in appreciation.

The impact that this game had, not only on football, but on sports television, was boundless. *Sports Illustrated* immediately labeled it "the best football game ever played." Perhaps it wasn't all that, but those who were at the Stadium that December day, as the light faded and the players whaled away at each other, would not soon forget it. Neither would the millions who thrilled to it on TV.

Having put four straight pennant victories together, Stengel pointed to a fifth flag in 1959. But this time around Al Lopez, always trailing after the New Yorkers, brought the White Sox home in front, thus denying Casey still another pennant. Such deprivation

PREVIOUS PAGES: ANOTHER VIEW FROM THE CENTER-FIELD BLEACHERS, THIS ONE TAKEN IN THE EARLY 1960S.
LEFT: YANKEE STADIUM FROM ABOVE DURING THE 1956 SEASON, PAINTED BY NEW YORK ARTIST ANDY JURINKO IN 1989.

ABOVE : GIANTS VERSUS COLTS ACTION. OPPOSITE: THE NEW YORK GIANTS CRUSHED THE CHICAGO BEARS 47–7 IN THE 1956 NFL CHAMPIONSHIP GAME. QUARTERBACK CHARLIE CONERLY, ON THE RIGHT, COMPLETED SEVEN OF TEN PASSES. ONE OF HIS TWO TOUCHDOWN PASSES CONNECTED WITH FRANK GIFFORD, SEEN HERE CELEBRATING THE WIN. FOLLOWING PAGES: ALEX WEBSTER IS SEEN HERE WEDGING INTO THE END ZONE FOR A TOUCHDOWN IN THE SECOND QUARTER.

record, because "he's got more power than Stalin." Casey was inclined to spout a lot of gobbledygook, but in a matter of months he looked like Nostradamus.

The World Series of 1960 came first, however. It evolved into one of the most preposterous and compelling group of postseason games ever played. Maris hit two homers against Pittsburgh, Mantle had three, and Skowron hit two. As a team, the Yankees hit .338, won games by scores of 16–3, 10–0, and 12–0, yet lost the Series in seven games!

In this Series the Pirates, a long shot to beat the Yankees, led the world in resiliency. They also had considerable help from Roberto Clemente, pitcher Vern Law, and outfielder Bill Virdon. In the ninth inning of the seventh game at Pittsburgh, they got a home run off the bat of Bill Mazeroski, to capture the championship. Bill's blow marked the only time a Series ever ended in a home run and probably sealed the doom of the old man at the helm of the Yankees.

Not long after Mazeroski's rocket disappeared over Berra's head in left field, the Yankees informed Casey they had no more use for his idiosyncratic services. At a crowded press conference in New York's Savoy Hilton Hotel, Dan Topping broke the news about Stengel's departure, emphasizing that many people thought the club was idiotic to sign him a dozen years before and now it was being assailed for getting rid of him. More cranky than ever, Casey refused to acknowledge that he was resigning because of advanced age. He preferred to be blunt about the Yankees' decision. "I was fired," he grumbled. "I'll never make the mistake of being seventy again."

Two weeks after Casey's exit, the sixty-five-year-old George Weiss also got his walking papers, as the Yankees again stressed they were hell-bent on a youth movement. Waiting in the wings was a tough, bona fide World War II hero, Major Ralph Houk, who had also been a part-time catcher for New York. Houk was a popular choice with the players to take over as manager. In the war, Houk had been through his share of

was cured in 1960, when Stengel, at seventy, had himself another winner, mainly thanks to some prodigious home run clouting by Mantle with 40, Moose Skowron with 26, and 39 by a crew-cut fellow named Roger Maris, who would have much preferred spending his summers back in Fargo, North Dakota.

Maris came to the Yankees from Kansas City in the winter of 1959, in a trade that saw Don Larsen and Hank Bauer depart for KC, in exchange for Maris and several others. The key man turned out to be Maris. Within a year, he had won the American League Most Valuable Player Award, as he showed signs of being the archetypal left-handed pull hitter. Stengel volunteered that Roger was certainly a candidate to break Ruth's

bombardment, but he was scarcely prepared for the season-long cannonading that was about to emanate from the bats of Maris and Mantle.

Even the most prescient of observers couldn't have predicted the 1961 home run scenario that took place between the two Yankee sluggers. When the battle was concluded, Maris and Mantle, almost pantomiming Ruth and Gehrig, had 115 home runs between them—61 for Roger, 54 for Mickey. The thrilling competition started in relatively slow motion, as Maris didn't hit his first home run until game 11. It wasn't until May 17 that Maris hit his first circuit shot at the Stadium, in game 29. Then Roger got into a groove: In the next 38 games he hit 24 home runs, in a matter of five weeks' time.

By June 22, Maris had 27 homers and Mickey had 22. Questions buzzed around Roger's short-cropped head. Can you beat the Babe? Do you deserve to beat the Babe? The pestering monotony of reporters' queries sometimes seemed to put more of a load on Maris than the actual assault on baseball's most cherished record.

I saw the stadium for the first time in the All-Star Game of 1960, when Willie Mays returned to New York for the day. I felt the same way I always had in visiting a stadium for the first time. I looked first at right field to see how far it was down the line-309, I believe-then to right center, and then tried to figure out the prevailing wind. I then checked out the grass around first base and the infield dirt, how the infield was groomed and where the sun would be at game time. I admit that I was surprised about the white shirts in the stands on game day. It made the ball hard to pick up around the infield.

Bill White,
former first-baseman,
Yankee announcer, and
ex-president of the
National League

Through the All-Star break, the two Yankees ran neck and neck, as Mantle put on his own pressure. On July 19, Roger had 35 home runs. Mantle had 33. By August 22, Roger had hit his 50th homer. In 1927, the Babe hadn't arrived at that figure until September 4. By early September, Mickey had moved closer, by hitting his 51st to Maris's 53rd. But Mickey's season was then put at risk with a sore forearm. At the same time, the pressure on Roger had become so acute that his hair started to fall out in clumps.

With 20 games to go, Maris needed 4 home runs to tie the Babe's record and 5 to break it. It ended, of course, with Roger passing the Sacrosanct Sixty, with his asterisked 61st homer on October 1, 1961, in the final game of the year at Yankee Stadium. (Since Maris didn't accomplish the feat in 154 games, as Ruth had, Commissioner Ford Frick decreed that it wasn't quite kosher, thus the pesky asterisk.)

On the day that Roger broke the record, some 23,000 fans showed up at the Stadium. Since the Yanks had already won the pennant, their presence was due mainly to witness Roger's bid.

In the fourth inning, facing Tracy Stallard of the Red Sox, Maris hit a ball that disappeared into the lower right-field stands, section 33. As the crowd roared, Roger began his triumphant jog around the bases. As he trotted past third base, he encountered a young fan who had trespassed on the field in order to congratulate the conquering hero. A phalanx of teammates clustered around Maris as he touched home plate. When Roger had hit his 60th homer a few days before, against Baltimore at the Stadium, he had been reluctant to wave to the fans from the dugout steps. Now he smiled broadly, an unemotional man who had realized what he had done and was, for the moment, savoring it. He took several bows, waved his cap at the fans, then retired to the bench. Of Roger's 61 home runs, 30 had been banged in his home ball park.

Later, as the baseball world joined in celebrating Roger's achievement, he said he wasn't going to take any walks in that final game. "I was going down swinging," he said. "Oddly, it was the first 1–0 game that I ever won with a homer."

What Maris had competed against—the robust ghost of the Babe and the popularity of Mickey—cost him much emotional turmoil in that fateful year of 1961. In the end he had triumphed—and that says much about a man who never sought the headlines.

The World Series that followed Maris's historic blast was anticlimactic. Houk turned out to be every bit the genius that the departed Stengel had been, as he managed the Yankees to a five-game victory over Cincinnati. As a freshman pilot, Houk joined Bucky Harris of Washington and Eddie Dyer of the Cardinals as the only pilots ever to corral all the marbles in their first season. As for Roger, he suffered something of a letdown, though he still came through to win the third game of the Series with a home run. Mantle was hardly a factor, for a hip injury kept him out of most of the Series.

In the hullabaloo over Maris, Whitey Ford's 14 innings of shutout pitching against the Reds almost went unnoticed. With 32 straight scoreless innings of Series pitching, Whitey had surpassed—yes—Babe Ruth, who had held the record for over forty years. As writer Don Honig noted, it had been a very bad year for Mr. Ruth.

ABOVE: ON AUGUST 13, 1960, WHITEY FORD PITCHED A THREE-HIT, 1–0 SHUTOUT AGAINST THE WASHINGTON SENATORS. HE DIDN'T ALLOW A HIT UNTIL ONE WAS OUT IN THE SEVENTH INNING. A YEAR LATER HE WON TWENTY GAMES FOR THE FIRST TIME IN HIS CAREER, AND SET A WORLD SERIES RECORD FOR CONSECUTIVE SHUTOUT INNINGS.

I rooted for the Pirates against the Yanks in the 1960 World Series, when I was studying at the Juilliard School of Music in New York City. I didn't know any better. My classmates, who were all Yankee fans, almost killed me when I cheered out loud at Bill Mazeroski's home run. Later, I became a diehard Yankee fan. Each time I went to Yankee Stadium, I admired the way Mickey Mantle ran and slid. The form was always so right, a real artist.

**Itzhak Perlman,
world-famous violinist**

Supporting the adage that the more things change, the more they remain the same, the Yankees, in 1962, found themselves in a World Series with the Giants, their old rivals, flashing back to the years of John McGraw and Leo Durocher. This time, the Giants were the San Francisco version but with Willie Mays still a considerable part of the Giants environment. The Series went to seven games, and if Willie McCovey's ninth-inning line drive at second-baseman Bobby Richardson had been a foot or so higher in that last contest, the Giants, and not the Yankees, would have emerged as champs.

The next year, as Maris and Mantle performed more like mortals than immortals (there were only 38 homers between them), the Yankees won the pennant again, mainly because of first-rate pitching. But in the World Series, it was the first-rate pitching of the transplanted Los Angeles Dodgers that did them in in four straight, the first time that New York had ever suffered such ignominy. Sandy Koufax of the Dodgers struck out 15 Yankees in the first game at the Stadium, as a record-breaking Series crowd of 69,000 rubbed their eyes in amazement. So overwhelming was Koufax's performance that Jim Hearn, the former Giants pitcher, who was an observer in the press box, insisted that the game had been "boring." Sandy was equally

boring in the fourth game, when he defeated Ford for the second time to sew up the title for Los Angeles. Aside from Sandy's excellence, the high point of the Series was a monstrous double to center field hit by Los Angeles' Frank Howard in the first game. Many testify that it was the longest fly ball ever hit within the confines of the Stadium.

Less than two months after the end of the Series, President John F. Kennedy was assassinated in Dallas. On the Sunday after Kennedy's tragic death a pro football game was scheduled to be played at Yankee Stadium between the Giants and the St. Louis Cardinals. There was speculation that the National Football League might cancel this and all the other games on that lugubrious afternoon. But the powers-that-be opted for the games to go on, suggesting disingenuously that Kennedy himself would have wanted it that way.

It was also thought that many might stay away from the Stadium, under the circumstances. When the game began, however, the ball park was jammed, even including a thousand or so standees. Perhaps it was one way for people to escape the numbing sadness being played out at home on television sets. A writer, Stanley Cohen, who chose to attend the game that day, explained his own presence this way: "Not often does one have the chance to experience a sense of deep communion with strangers, to be part of a huge throng and know that each unfamiliar face is expressing, in its own way, some part of what you yourself feel. . . . The crowd seemed to have little interest in the outcome and when the game ended there was that awful hush, a flat feeling."

In 1964, the Yankees pursued a fifth straight American League flag. They would have to do it without the guidance on the field of Houk, who was promoted to general manager. The gentleman named to succeed Houk was Berra. Certainly the choice was popular with the fans, for nobody had ever been located who

ABOVE: ROGER MARIS BROKE BABE RUTH'S SINGLE-SEASON HOME RUN RECORD IN 1961, WHILE ENDURING THE DEMANDS OF THE NEW YORK MEDIA AS WELL AS THE FREQUENT SUGGESTION THAT IF ANYONE HAD THE RIGHT TO BETTER THE BABE'S MARK IT SHOULD BE MICKEY MANTLE.

I grew up a Yankees fan despite never having been east of the Mississippi. When I finally made it from South Dakota to New York, it dawned on me that the same subway that took me to midtown and the movies could transport me to a place I actually thought at first was made up. I've never gotten over that heart-stopping moment when the gray-and-metal outsides of subway and city crack open to reveal the green. And the secret of Yankee Stadium, I see now, is that it was a piece of the prairie—my childhood—set down in the great big, confusing city that became my home.

Elinor Nauen,
editor of *Diamonds Are a*
Girl's Best Friend: Women
Writers on Baseball

disliked the man or the maxims that had been credited to him.

Berra and his team struggled during the year. At one stage, Yogi actually lost his temper, a historic first for him. After a particularly bad loss, Phil Linz, a utility infielder who played his harmonica about as well as the famous Stan Musial, decided to play a few riffs on his instrument on the team bus. Yogi objected to such flightiness, demanding that Linz cease his concert. When Linz kept playing, a shouting match ensued, with Yogi making an imprudent suggestion about where Phil could stuff his harmonica.

Whether there was any cause or effect, the Yankees perked up in the pennant stretch drive, beating out the White Sox by a single game to win their fifth straight flag for the second time. In the World Series that followed, the Yankees lost to the Cardinals in seven exciting games, as St. Louis's aggressive right-hander, Bob Gibson, won two games and struck out 31. Mantle had three home runs, and Maris had one, but catcher Tim McCarver and outfielder Lou Brock had 20 hits between them and 10 runs batted in to lead the way for St. Louis.

The 1964 season and the World Series that followed reflected a changing and volatile era in America. The Cardinals were heavily stocked with a group of dynamic black players, while many of the Yankees stars were in decline. Only one regular on the Yankees, Howard, was black. On a more ironic level, the brilliant Gibson turned out to be the ultimate clutch player and pitcher in the Cards lineup, thus defying the bigoted notion that black players were incapable of coping with game pressure.

The Series had been dramatic, from start to finish. But that was nothing compared with what transpired after the final out. On the grounds that he had not maintained adequate control over his former buddies, Berra was dismissed as manager. The Cards manager, Johnny Keane, beat his own front office to the punch by resigning, after he had heard rumors that he was going to be jettisoned despite his Series victory. Mirabile dictu, Keane was hired at once by the Yankees to replace Berra!

If Keane thought he was escaping further unpleasantness in St. Louis by coming to the home of perennial champions, he was bound to be disappointed. In August 1964, Columbia Broadcasting System (CBS) bought the Yankees for a record $11.2 million, with high hopes that the team would continue their domination of the game. But Keane was confronted with a roster dotted with aging, injured stars, and suddenly the Yankees were failing to find proper replacements. The Yankees also had to cope with the free-agent draft and the strategies of interleague trading. Compounding their difficulties, the new team in town, the lowly Mets, having hired Stengel as manager in a shrewd public relations coup, were outdrawing the Yankees by almost a half-million fans.

By 1965, the Yankees had plummeted to sixth place, as Minnesota won the pennant. CBS then assigned Mike Burke, a singularly eclectic and colorful individual, to preside over the further disintegration of the franchise. When Burke became president of the

Yanks, in 1966, many of the club's veterans were gulping Ovaltine and the farm system was rotting away. There was little that Burke could do to stem the decline. He boasted a glorious curriculum vitae: former Penn halfback, intrepid World War II special agent, ex-circus impresario, video executive. All this, and a haircut that looked like something out of King Arthur's Roundtable.

But Burke had not grown up in baseball, a peculiar institution that could put more experienced men than Mike to shame. Ironically, since Burke had credentials more in promotion than in the assessment of baseball talent, who could have anticipated that he would commit an egregious public relations blunder?

As the 1966 season came to a disastrous end, with the Yankees finishing dead last for the first time in over fifty years, Burke imprudently fired Red Barber, one of the shining broadcasting-booth adornments in the game. It was enough to make people forget that Burke had been responsible for getting the Metropolitan Opera star, Robert Merrill, to sing the National Anthem at Yankees games and luring the tiny baseball-loving poet Marianne Moore to throw out the first ball at an opening game.

Just what had Barber done to deserve losing his job as a Yankees broadcaster? He had made the "mistake" of discussing on air the pitifully small crowd on hand at the Stadium for a game with the White Sox near the end of the season.

"Judge Landis once said to me, 'report everything you see,'" explained Barber. What Barber saw that drizzly, foggy day at the Stadium was empty stands. So Red leaned into his TV mike and said, "I don't know what the paid attendance is today, but whatever it is it's the smallest crowd in the history of Yankee Stadium and the smallest crowd is the story, not the ball game."

Barber didn't rub it in; he let it go at that. He had said it, he had reported it. Later, when he was on the radio side, Barber announced the exact number of paying fans: 413.

A few days later, Burke rewarded Barber for his candor and honest reporting by dismissing him. A few years before that, Mel Allen, the popular "Voice of the Yankees," had been cashiered from his job in the booth. Now it was Barber. To this day the mystery of Allen's firing has not been explained to anybody's satisfaction. "Allen was a man of grace and integrity, a shameless huckster of charming originality," wrote Stephen Jay Gould a few days after Mel's death in June 1996.

The great names of Yankee baseball were now departing from the scene. Maris, never happy in New York, was traded to the St. Louis Cardinals after the '66 campaign; Ford, after one of baseball's most remarkable pitching records (236–106), retired at age thirty-eight in 1967; Mantle played out his final season in 1968, with his average down at .237 and his head down in despair. He hit his last Yankee Stadium homer against the Red Sox on September 20, 1968. He ended at 536 homers, not close to the Babe or even Willie Mays, but the conventional wisdom insisted that had he not been plagued with

The experience of playing in the cavernous Yankee Stadium for the first time, after I had just turned twenty-three, was truly overwhelming. I don't think I'd ever seen a baseball stadium that tall. But as Gene Mauch once said, "The way to beat guys is not to admire them," so we tried very hard to keep all that Yankee Stadium lore from intimidating us. Before the first game that the Cardinals played at the stadium in 1964, I worked on foul popups and I quickly discovered what a fine background the stadium provided for catchers. If you worked behind the bat, as I did, your depth perception was unusually good.

Tim McCarver, played for the St. Louis Cardinals against the Yankees in the 1964 World Series

PREVIOUS PAGES: ROGER MARIS'S QUEST IS ENDED. THIS PAINTING BY BILL PURDOM SHOWS THE YANKEE RIGHT-FIELDER CLOUTING HIS SIXTY-FIRST HOME RUN IN THE LAST GAME OF THE 1961 SEASON. IT WAS HIT AGAINST BOSTON RED SOX PITCHER TRACY STALLARD AND CAUGHT BY A FAN NAMED SAL DURANTE. IT ECLIPSED THE SINGLE-SEASON HOME RUN RECORD SET IN 1927 BY BABE RUTH. ABOVE: ILLUSTRATOR MARC SIMONT, WHOSE WORK APPEARED IN *SPORTS ILLUSTRATED* AND OTHER PUBLICATIONS, DEFERRED TO ROGER MARIS'S PULL-HITTING PROWESS BY STACKING THE OPPOSITION, AS WELL AS THE UMPIRES, IN FRONT OF THE RIGHT-FIELD GRANDSTAND. BELOW: SINCE 1951 THE YANKEES' PUBLIC ADDRESS ANNOUNCER HAS BEEN BOB SHEPPARD, A FORMER PROFESSOR OF PUBLIC SPEAKING AT ST. JOHN'S UNIVERSITY. BEFORE HIS YANKEE ASSIGNMENT, SHEPPARD WORKED BRIEFLY FOR THE BROOKLYN FOOTBALL DODGERS AT EBBETS FIELD, AND LATER FOR THE NEW YORK TITANS AT THE POLO GROUNDS. HE STILL WORKS FOR THE FOOTBALL GIANTS AT THE MEADOWLANDS, THUS COMPLETING TOURS OF DUTY AT FOUR NEW YORK AREA STADIUMS. OPPOSITE: ON MAY 22, 1963, MICKEY MANTLE HAMMERED A HOME RUN AGAINST THE KANSAS ATHLETICS THAT CLANGED AGAINST THE COPPER FRIEZE, JUST SIX FEET FROM THE TOP OF THE ROOF. IT'S THE CLOSEST ANYONE HAS COME TO HITTING A FAIR BALL OUT OF YANKEE STADIUM. A YANKEE PUBLICIST CALCULATED THAT THE BALL WOULD HAVE TRAVELED MORE THAN 600 FEET HAD IT NOT HIT THE ROOF.

injuries he might have surpassed one or both of them.

The rebuilding process moved forward under Houk, who was restored as manager after Keane left in 1966. After several mediocre years, Houk whipped the club home into second place, behind Baltimore, in 1970. New faces began to appear in the Yankee lineup, headed by Thurman Munson, a tough young catcher out of Ohio's Kent State. Munson quickly showed that he would be a fitting successor to those Yankee catching giants of the past: Dickey, Berra, and Howard. But Munson was not enough to push the Yankees past the Orioles and Oakland, both American League powers at this stage.

Outfielder Bobby Murcer, like Mantle an Oklahoman, had several fine seasons in the early 1970s, but the expectation that he'd be another Mickey was too

367 Feet

108 Ft. 1 In.

Has Anybody Ever Hit a Fair Ball Out of Yankee Stadium?

The answer is no. But several hitters have come close. Oddly, the Babe and Lou are not on that list. Mickey Mantle is.

On May 22, 1963, Mickey powered one off Kansas City right-hander Bill Fischer that some insist would still be traveling if it hadn't struck the façade in right field. Hit about 367 feet from home plate, the ball rocketed toward the stands on an orbital trajectory, at a 45-degree angle, traveling 103 feet above the ground. "The hardest ball I've ever hit," said Mickey. A one-time teammate of Mickey's, Joe Collins, once said, "Mickey hits every one like they don't count under four hundred feet."

Other challengers: Luke Easter of the Cleveland Indians hit a ball off the right-field roof in 1951, foul by only a few inches. Josh Gibson, playing in the Negro Leagues, once struck a ball past the left-field foul pole and out of the Stadium, according to legend. Unfortunately, there are no eyewitnesses around today to authenticate the story.

Other extraordinary pokes that didn't go foul: Hank Greenberg of the Detroit Tigers hit a cloud scraper to dead center, behind the flagpole, almost 500 feet away, but Joe DiMaggio was there to make a marvelous catch. Gehrig and Larry Doby of the Cleveland Indians both hit homers into the right-center bleachers, while DiMaggio and Greenberg also hit long homers into left-center. Perhaps the longest ball ever hit *within* the Stadium was Jimmie Foxx's blast off Lefty Gomez into the far reaches of the left-field stands in the 1930s.

LEFT: A BRIGHT OCTOBER AFTERNOON IS THE SETTING FOR THE FIRST GAME OF THE 1963 WORLD SERIES. MOST OF THE CROWD WENT HOME DISAPPOINTED AFTER THE DODGERS, BEHIND SANDY KOUFAX, WHO STRUCK OUT FIFTEEN BATTERS TO SET A SERIES RECORD, WON 5–2. THE DODGERS WON THE NEXT THREE GAMES, TO COMPLETE THE FIRST WORLD SERIES SWEEP OVER THE YANKEES SINCE 1922. ABOVE TOP: YANKEE STADIUM CAN BE REACHED BY TWO SUBWAY LINES; THE LEXINGTON AVENUE, WOODLAWN–JEROME AVENUE LINE IS SEEN HERE IN A PICTURE TAKEN JUST BEFORE THE SEASON BEGAN IN 1963. ABOVE BOTTOM: THE PROXIMITY OF A COMMUTER RAILROAD LINE TO YANKEE STADIUM IS EVIDENT IN THIS PICTURE TAKEN IN OCTOBER 1964. THE NEW YORK CENTRAL NO LONGER RUMBLES PAST THE STADIUM, BUT METRO NORTH'S HUDSON DIVISION DOES, SUGGESTING TO SOME THAT A STATION AT THIS LOCATION MIGHT PROVE FEASIBLE.

much to ask of him. Neither could the able right-hander Mel Stottlemyre hoist the team to another level.

While the club on the field was under repair, Burke, feeling that the Bronx was no longer a viable venue in which the Yanks could play ball, began casting a flirtatious eye at New Jersey. He appreciated the mystique and history of the Yankees and the Stadium, but acting under instructions from CBS, he felt it necessary to implicitly threaten to take the team else-

When I was thirteen years old, in 1965, my father, just thirty-seven, suffered a massive heart attack. It was touch-and-go for several weeks. He was away from work for two months but promised that when he was well enough, he'd take me to opening day at Yankee Stadium. It was the first thing we had done together outside the house or hospital since his illness. It was one of those crisp April days that you associate with the start of the baseball season. We sat in the lower stands in right field. In the bottom of the first inning, Mickey Mantle, batting left-handed against the Twins' Camilo Pascual, sent a shot into the upper deck in right. It soared directly above us and into a delirious crowd. Even in the huge ball park, you could distinctly hear the crack of the bat as Mickey made contact—baseball's version of a thunderclap. As Mickey rounded the bases, I remember holding up my scorecard and showing my dad how I was recording the home run. Oddly, as close as I followed Mantle through the years, and with the dozens of games I saw in person at Yankee Stadium, that was only one of three home runs he hit in games I attended.

**Bob Costas,
announcer**

where. After all, the Dodgers and Giants had thumbed their noses at New York over a decade before.

A deal was worked out, however, with Burke and New York's Mayor, John V. Lindsay, for the city to purchase Yankee Stadium from Rice University and the Knights of Columbus for $24 million. Under such a transaction, the Yankees would rent the premises from the city. (Rice had owned the Stadium, and the Knights of Columbus owned the grounds.)

There was much grousing about the nature of the

arrangement, mainly from those who didn't believe that public funds should be used to support a private enterprise. Critics charged that if CBS sought to have a plaything in the Yankees, they should pay for it. Others counterargued that the Stadium continued to mean a good deal to New Yorkers, not only for commercial reasons but as a boost to the public psyche.

By 1973, it was apparent that CBS wanted to divest itself of the problem. Toward that end, Gabe Paul, then vice president and general manager of the Cleveland Indians, brought Burke together with a wealthy Cleveland shipbuilder named George Steinbrenner, and the two men worked out a deal, along with other limited partners, to buy the Yankees. The sale was made for an estimated $10 million, presumably a loss of several million for CBS. At the time few had ever heard of Steinbrenner, who had studied Shakespeare at Williams and served briefly as a backfield coach at Purdue. But he would soon rectify that matter.

When the tumult died down, the city decided to proceed on a mass renovation of the House That Ruth Built at a cost that ultimately came to about $100 million. At first, it was felt that the job could be done for half of that. But that proved to be a fantasy. Because of the mayor's role, some newspaper pundits chose to call the edifice The House That Lindsay Rebuilt. During the period of renewal, the Yankees became the tenants of the Mets at Shea Stadium for the years of 1974 and 1975. There were no pennants to be won at Shea, although the Yanks challenged in the Eastern Division each year.

In 1967, the stadium had undergone something of a scrubbing and face-lifting at a cost of $2 million. But now the modernization—which included a change of color from muted green to white paint on the exterior and a rich, deep blue on the seats, pillars, and interior—put fans on notice that a new era at the Stadium was about to dawn.

With the reconstruction, completed before the

ABOVE LEFT: RED BARBER'S EASY RAPPORT WITH PLAYERS IS EVIDENT IN THIS PICTURE TAKEN WHILE RED INTERVIEWED YANKEE FIRST-BASEMAN JOE COLLINS. ABOVE RIGHT: RED BARBER ESTABLISHED HIS PREEMINENCE AS A BROADCASTER WITH THE DODGERS, THEN JOINED THE YANKEES IN 1954 AFTER A DISAGREEMENT WITH DODGER PRESIDENT WALTER O'MALLEY. HE REMAINED WITH THE YANKEES THROUGH THE 1966 SEASON. "THE RADIO ANNOUNCER IS THE SUPREME, THE COMPLETE ARTIST," HE SAID. "YOU PAINT THE PICTURE. . . . AND THAT IS SATISFYING TO THE HUMAN EGO." RIGHT: IN 1968, DURING THE BRIEF BUT IMAGINATIVE MIKE BURKE–CBS OWNERSHIP REIGN, THE POET MARIANNE MOORE, A BASEBALL DEVOTEE, WAS IN-VITED TO THROW OUT THE FIRST BALL OF THE SEASON. SHE RE-QUESTED, AND WAS GRANTED, PERMISSION TO VISIT THE STADIUM A DAY EARLY TO PRACTICE. SEATED AT MOORE'S LEFT IS BETTE HOUK, THE WIFE OF THE YANKEE MANAGER.

1976 season began, the capacity of the big house was reduced to a more human scale of 55,000. Two-thirds of the bleacher seats were eliminated, leaving only 2,500 or so of the cheaper pews. The three-foot fences in the outfield were gone, and left-center Death Valley, the source of so much folklore, no longer existed. Be-fore the renovation the center-field monuments and plaques—to Gehrig, Huggins, and the Babe—were in fair territory, in the deepest part of the park. Now they were behind fences. No longer was it possible for dis-tant flies to be pursued in that area.

Above the bleacher seats rose the three-paneled scoreboard. Above that was the traditional Yankee symbol of the scalloped valance. All of the 118 grand-stand columns that had once obstructed a decent view of Yankee icons had been removed. The largest Louisville Slugger bat in the universe, a 138-foot stain-less steel and fiberglass smokestack, sprang up near the

The old stadium had a biblical look. I assumed it had been standing on 161st Street since before Christ. Years later, when I saw the actual Roman Coliseum, I couldn't suppress an inner gasp of recognition. Ahhh! It's like Yankee Stadium.

Laura Cunningham,
in her novel *Sleeping
Arrangements*

main entrance. King Kong, at the peak of his powers, couldn't have brandished this weapon against the pitchers of the world. A wide pedestrian plaza, where one could buy food and tickets, faced a four-story parking garage, which could accommodate over 2,300 cars. The lambent old ball palace and the adjoining Bronx neighborhood, run down after fifty years, seemed to come alive again. But criticism still focused on the issue that not enough had been done on the stores, houses, and playgrounds near Yankee Stadium. This condition still remains a flashpoint for controversy.

Upon his arrival in New York, Steinbrenner, a true Yankee Doodle Dandy who was born on the Fourth of July, boldly announced that he hadn't joined the Yankees to fail, the siren song of most incoming sports executives. He also promised, however, that he wouldn't be very active in the day-to-day operation of the ball club. Steinbrenner apparently

PREVIOUS PAGES: REMODELING IS UNDER WAY AS JOE DIMAGGIO POSES ON THE IRT SUBWAY PLATFORM, NO DOUBT PONDERING PAST GLORIES. LEFT: NEW YORK MAYOR JOHN LINDSAY IS AT THE CONTROLS OF THE BULLDOZER IN THIS PUBLICITY SHOT, TAKEN AS WORKERS BEGAN THE DEMOLITION JOB. BOTTOM: THE RENOVATION IS NEARLY COMPLETE IN THIS PICTURE, TAKEN DURING THE WINTER OF 1975–76. SEATS ARE MISSING, AS IS THE SCOREBOARD, BUT THE PLAYING FIELD APPEARS READY FOR ACTION.

didn't understand himself well, for he turned out, in short order, to be a hands-on fellow, whether he was dealing for ballplayers or stockpiling tuna fish sandwiches for lunch. He was seemingly concerned about everything from the toothbrushes used by his janissaries to their tonsorial habits.

Although many have been critical of Steinbrenner for his often intemperate, boorish behavior and for his unwelcome intrusions into the managing process, he could also be humane and generous on occasion. Non-admirers facetiously said of him that he was a man of "untold civic virtue and quiet altruism." But there was no tongue-in-cheek when it was suggested that he got things done. Headlines and newsprint were as vital to him as the oxygen he breathed, but he was also a chronic fan of the Yankees. He wanted to win badly, and if it took opening up his private vault to achieve that end, he would do it.

Starting in 1974, when Catfish Hunter, the Cy Young Award right-hander of the Oakland Athletics, became a free agent after owner Charles Finley breached his contract, Steinbrenner plunged joyously into the market with his checkbook. Almost every front office in baseball was in hot pursuit of Catfish, but it was Steinbrenner who nailed him. The complicated deal for Catfish's services featured enough codicils to baffle a battery of tax lawyers—but it ended up being worth about $2.85 million to him, then an unheard-of sum in the baseball world.

Hunter went on to win 23 games in his first year, not enough to restore first-place glory, but a sign that things were looking up in the Bronx. With the acquisition of Hunter, Steinbrenner put the baseball panjandrums on notice that he was willing to spend and spend to win and win.

But he also decided it was time to jettison his manager, the mild-mannered Bill Virdon, whose demeanor was quite in variance with that of his owner. Halfway through the 1975 season, Steinbrenner fired Virdon and embarked on his first adventure with Billy Martin

as manager. Steinbrenner had long cherished the combativeness of Billy Martin, and his instinct was that Billy would restore the Yankees to the heights with his toughness and drive. Martin had just lost his job as Texas manager and was eager to get back into the fray. Steinbrenner sent an emissary out to Colorado, where Billy was doing some trout fishing and, in this instance, George caught his own fish. Martin's new assignment with the Yankees was something he might have dreamed about when he was an embattled, big-nosed little kid growing up in a lower-middle-class neighborhood of West Berkeley, California.

Returning from their tenancy at Shea Stadium, the Yankees were goaded and dragooned by Martin into a pennant in his first full year as pilot. In a tension-filled playoff series with Kansas City, the Yankees ended up winning the American League flag for the first time in a dozen years. The coup de grace was delivered in the ninth inning of the fifth game, when Chris Chambliss hit the first pitch from Mark Littell into the right-field stands. The capacity crowd at Yankee Stadium went wild, as Chambliss gamboled around the bases. It was a collective roar that hadn't been heard on those premises for years.

"People had forgotten what it meant to root for the Yankees," remarked Martin, as he prepared to face the Cincinnati Reds in the World Series.

But the Reds, a powerful and determined ball club that only the year before had won a tumultuous World Series from Boston, were not about to be taken in by Billy's pugnacity. They swept the Yanks in four straight, a major embarrassment to both Billy and his boss. After the final out at Yankee Stadium, Billy, who had been ejected from the game, sat in his office and wept.

The defeat at the hands of the Reds sent the disappointed Steinbrenner in search of more high-priced talent. Over 2 million fans attended games at the Stadium in 1976, but that, and a pennant, didn't salve Steinbrenner's feelings. He

PREVIOUS PAGES: On April 15, 1976, the renovated Yankee Stadium opened to more than 54,000 spectators, who watched the Yanks beat the Minnesota Twins 11–4. ABOVE: Although the fans are still not sure, Chris Chambliss and teammates Thurman Munson and Sandy Alomar are leaping for joy at the certainty that Chambliss's drive is headed for the grandstand, delivering the 1976 pennant for the Yankees in the ninth inning of the fifth ALCS playoff game against the Kansas City Royals. Spectators engulfed the field seconds later, forcing Chambliss to seek the safety of the clubhouse before he was able to finish circling the bases. When the field was finally cleared, he came back out and registered the winning run. BELOW: Thurman Munson, the Yankee captain, blocks the plate against the Milwaukee Brewers' George Scott in a game played in September 1976. Scott was a huge man, and the sight of him charging down the baseline might have given a lesser man some pause. Munson's cool expression shows not a hint of trepidation. FOLLOWING PAGES: In the sixth game of the 1977 World Series, Yankee outfielder Reggie Jackson hammered three consecutive homers on three pitches from three different Los Angeles Dodgers pitchers. This is the first, against Burt Hooton. Jackson's heroics nailed the first Yankee world championship since 1962. "Babe Ruth was great," Jackson said later, "I'm just lucky."

signed Cincinnati's free-agent southpaw Don Gullett, who had won one of the games in the Series rout of the Yankees—and paid over $2 million for the privilege. The injury-plagued Gullett turned out to be less important to the team's fortunes than the development of a wiry little Cajun left-hander, Ron Guidry.

In the winter of 1976, however, Steinbrenner pursued the thirty-one-year-old Reggie Jackson, a prodigious slugger for Oakland and Baltimore. With the tenacity of Javert, the Yankees owner hustled after Jackson, flashing his own considerable charm, his pocketbook, and his acquaintance with headwaiters in the most posh restaurants. The two men even walked the streets of New York's Upper East Side together, and Reggie didn't mind at all that people recognized him. A complicated, intelligent, articulate athlete, Reggie also was more than a little obsessed with himself. His main religion, aside from money and cars, was self-promotion—and he was mighty good at that. Yet, with an ego higher than Abe Lincoln's stovepipe hat, Reggie could also produce. He had proved that he was a winning ballplayer, with enormous all-round talent. That's what Steinbrenner wanted him for. So the Yankees landed Jackson, awarding him a five-year contract that guaranteed him almost $3 million a year.

Inevitably, the coming of Reggie to New York

I'll always remember my first Series at the stadium in 1951. I can still see the final out, a line drive by Sal Yvars of the Giants, caught in right field by Hank Bauer. I remember it because Yvars was a pinch hitter, so I had to introduce him. But my top memory was Don Larsen's perfect game in 1956. Next, of course, was Reggie's three homers in the final game of 1977.

Bob Sheppard, public address announcer for the Yankees through eighteen World Series

roiled the waters in the Yankee clubhouse. Even before his arrival, Reggie predicted that a candy bar would be named after him if he came to the Big Town. He may have had the popular Baby Ruth confection in mind, although he was probably unaware that the sweet was named for President Grover Cleveland's daughter, not the Yankees' Babe. Then, early in the season, an article appeared in *Sport* magazine, in which Reggie declared diffidently, "I'm the straw that stirs the drink." Not letting well enough alone, he added that Munson, the team's prickly leader, could only stir it "bad." Munson couldn't have been expected to react kindly to such deprecation. Their relationship never healed.

From the start, Martin, the angry mentor of the pin-striped Bronx Zoo, as it was now called by the press, didn't much care for Jackson. That made it almost unanimous. Billy hadn't been consulted in the signing of Jackson, and that also continued to stick in his craw. It was just a matter of time before Martin would explode. Such an episode took place before a national television audience, as the Yanks played the Red Sox at Fenway Park. Martin suddenly confronted Reggie in the dugout, accusing him of loafing on a ball hit into his area. It appeared that the two men were about to come to blows, but cooler heads prevailed. The two antagonists, like scorpions in a bottle, were pulled apart by Elston Howard and Yogi Berra.

Having witnessed the event on television, Steinbrenner made up his mind on the spot to jettison Martin. Because of the surprising intercession of Reggie himself, however, Steinbrenner failed to follow through on his impulse. It wasn't magnanimity that persuaded Reggie to make the case in Billy's behalf. Rather, it was that he appreciated what an iconic personality Martin was in New York and he decided not to be responsible for his manager's guillotining.

Meanwhile, there was a pennant race to be fought and won. The Yankees were much more than a vaudeville act somewhat out of control; they were honest-to-goodness pennant contenders. And Reggie, the "Hamlet in double knits," as Red Smith called him, was playing a substantial role. At the end of the year, Reggie had 32 home runs and 110 runs batted in, although he did strike out 129 times in 525 at-bats.

The flag race went down to the wire and for the second straight year the Yankees confronted Kansas City in the playoff. The Yankees rallied to win at Kansas City in the ninth inning of the fifth game, thus earning the right to play the Los Angeles Dodgers in the World Series. Without a Series victory since 1962, an atypical drought for New York, Steinbrenner thirsted for the long-delayed triumph. He would get it—with the help of one of the most dynamic one-man shows in the history of the Series. And it was Reggie, indeed, who was "the straw that stirred the drink."

As the Yanks moved ahead, three games to two, Reggie warmed up for his magnum opus by hitting a home run on Saturday in Los Angeles, then another one in his last time at bat on Sunday, also in the Dodgers' ball yard. With the scene shifting to Yankee Stadium on Tuesday, October 18, for the sixth game, a full house of 56,000 witnessed a performance unequaled in seventy-four World Series.

In the second inning, Reggie walked and scored ahead of a homer by Chris Chambliss. The score was tied. In the fourth inning, Reggie came to bat with Munson on base and Los Angeles ahead, 3–2. He hit the first pitch from Burt Hooton on a blazing line into the seats in right field, putting the Yanks in the lead, 4–3, and knocking Hooton out of the box.

With a runner on base in the fifth inning, Reggie hit Elias Sosa's first pitch again into the old Ruthville enclave. The Yankees now led, 7–3. As the leadoff batter in the eighth, Reggie could have been replaced by Martin for a defensive player like Paul Blair. But when do they replace the star performer in the last act? This time, again on the first pitch, Reggie belted Charlie Hough's knuckle-ball delivery over 450 feet in dead center, an area that was unoccupied by fans in order to

My own feelings about Yankee Stadium crowds are mixed. None of this, however, has much to do with the Yankee Stadium fans' enthusiasm for their players—a screeching, passionate, hilarious extroversion that, if decibels are a fair gauge, equals, or perhaps surpasses, any other local loyalty in the game.

Roger Angell,
in *Late Innings*, 1978

give batters a decent background. The crowd got to its feet, en masse, roaring in appreciation and disbelief. Yes, the Babe had hit three homers in a Series game twice, in 1926 and 1928, but never three in a row, and never on three consecutive pitches.

"I must admit when Reggie hit his third home run and I was sure nobody was listening, I applauded into my glove," Steve Garvey, the Dodgers' first-baseman, later acknowledged.

In his last nine at-bats in a Series that he had totally dominated, Jackson hit five home runs, made six hits, scored seven times, and proved that, for all of his rampant narcissism, he was the player of the hour.

What could Reggie possibly do for an encore in 1978? Well, as Al Jolson, the old Swanee singer of vaudeville, used to boast, "You ain't seen nuthin' yet."

This time, however, the fireworks were of a different nature. Because Billy had tried to recast Reggie into the role of designated hitter, their relationship worsened. Jackson became a brooder and appeared depressed. Martin merely remained sullen.

Though Ron Guidry was having a year that ended in 25–3 and other pitchers like Sparky Lyle, Goose Gossage, and Ed Figueroa tried to keep the Yankees in the race, by July 17 the New Yorkers were 14 games behind the Red Sox. All of this was mere subplot to the interminable Mack Sennett comedy that infected the Yankees front office. Steinbrenner fought with Martin, Billy fought with Al Rosen, the former Cleveland

To me the glacial territory of Yankee Stadium is a Siberia for the novelistic soul. Though championship flags abound, the place is desolate and icy. The armies of Russia rumble through its winter midnights. The stadium is witless, vulgar, and ugly. To watch it demolished would be like seeing Marxism die, but replaced, no doubt, by the granite of poverty, its neighborhood overflowing onto its empty space, searching helplessly for home.

Jonathan Schwartz,
musicologist and
Red Sox fan

third-baseman who had been hired as the team's president, and Billy fought, naturally, with Reggie.

The climactic event occurred at the Stadium on the night of July 17, 1978. The Yanks were tied with Kansas City in the last of the tenth inning, when Munson reached first base safely, with none out. It was Reggie's turn to bat. He had failed to get a hit in his first four appearances, and now Billy signaled for him to bunt the potential winning run to second base. Jackson, who had not been called on to bunt all year, regarded such an instruction as lèse-majesté, an insult to his imperial presence.

The first pitch was too high to bunt. But Reggie had moved into the bunt posture, thus revealing his intentions to the KC infielders. Figuring that KC sensed that a bunt was imminent, Martin removed the bunt sign. But seething over the slight, Jackson continued to try to bunt. He fouled off three attempts and was declared out for his efforts. In the dugout Martin was barely able to suppress his rage. A player didn't ignore his orders. If the player was Reggie, that made insubordination even worse.

LEFT: FIVE-TIME ALL STAR THIRD-BASEMAN GRAIG NETTLES PLAYED FOR THE YANKEES FROM 1973 THROUGH 1983, AND MADE ACROBATIC PLAYS ALMOST ROUTINELY. HE'S SEEN HERE SPEARING A LINE DRIVE HIT BY JIM ESSIAN OF THE OAKLAND A'S IN A GAME PLAYED IN 1980.

It was a sunny, dry September Sunday–the kind of day that can convince an unsuspecting stranger that New York is a wonderful place to spend the summer. That Sunday had been declared Catfish Hunter Day. Ole Catfish was retiring and New York had turned out for him at the stadium. Maybe it was in comparison with the parched browns of Israel at summer's end. Maybe it was the smell of hot dogs drifting over the stands. All I know for sure is that when I emerged from the tunnel and stood there in the first tier, looking over home base, I gasped at the perfect greenness of it. So this was a diamond. . . . It was the perfect American day, the perfect American place, the perfect American sentence (just delivered by Catfish, who had said, "Thank you, God, for giving me strength and making me a ballplayer").

**Lesley Hazleton,
from *Diamonds Are a Girl's Best Friend,* a collection
by Elinor Nauen**

As a result of the incident, Reggie was suspended for five days. But Martin still wasn't placated. When Reggie returned to active duty, Martin unleashed a verbal attack on Reggie. "He's a born liar," screeched Billy. But he didn't stop at Reggie. He went on to remind people that Steinbrenner had been "convicted." Digging up the Watergate-related conviction was a sore point in Steinbrenner's background. It underlined just how self-destructive Billy could be.

The next day Martin resigned, to be replaced by former Cleveland pitcher Bob Lemon, a taciturn fellow who knew all about the Yankees from his past experience constantly finishing in second place behind them.

"The team has a shot at the pennant, and I hope they win it" was Martin's bittersweet valedictory.

But this didn't end the latest melodrama being played out at the Stadium. Not at all. Five days later,

in an episode almost defying belief, the Yankees announced at Old-Timers Day at the Stadium that Billy would be returning as Yankees manager in two years. Public address announcer Bob Sheppard's stunning words set off a roar of approval from the 46,711 fans, as Billy waved his cap at the multitudes.

Behind the scenes, Billy had supposedly apologized to Steinbrenner, who had never stopped admiring Billy for his hard-nosed managing and his apparent grip on the affections of many Yankee fans.

For the rest of the '78 season, Lemon quietly attended to matters. What had been a battlefield in the Yankee clubhouse now became a veritable sea of tranquillity. That's precisely what Rosen had bargained for when he brought Lemon in to quell the mutinous atmosphere.

In a remarkable turnabout, the Yankees—aided by a healthy Mickey Rivers, second-baseman Willie Randolph, and Catfish Hunter—broke out in a rash of victories. Of their last 68 games they won 48. Their comeback featured a four-game destruction of the Red Sox in Fenway Park in September, thus setting up a one-game playoff for the American League East title at Fenway on Monday, October 2. In 1948, Cleveland had licked the Red Sox in a similar playoff game at Fenway. Once again, in 1978, the widely heralded Curse of the Bambino undermined the Red Sox, or at least so the superstition-laden Bosox fans insisted.

In a dramatic finish, the Yanks emerged 5–4 victors over the Red Sox, propelled by a three-run home run by Bucky Dent, their normally light-hitting shortstop. Bucky's serendipitous blow transformed him overnight into a Yankee idol. His dark-haired good looks also didn't hurt him at all with the feminine clientele.

The last-minute comeback in Boston thrust the Yanks into still another playoff confrontation with Kansas City, with the first two games to be played on the foreign field. Already anointed as "Mr. October" and glorying in the role, Jackson reduced KC to a shambles in the four-game series. He began his bombardment in the first game with a three-run homer and two other hits, then added another homer later in the series. He finished with six runs batted in and a .462 average. KC's third-baseman George Brett couldn't hide his frustration. "They're the best team money can buy," he grumbled. "They have a lot of players who play their best under pressure."

Brett practically predicted the future. In the World Series against the New Yorkers, the Dodgers took a quick two-game lead, before play resumed at the Stadium. From that point on, the Yankees took charge.

They swept the next three games at Yankee Stadium and one more game at LA. In this mission, their twenty-second World Series win in thirty-two appearances, they received considerable help from Graig Nettles' acrobatics at third base and an appropriate measure of October thunder from Reggie, who had two homers and eight runs batted in.

With two straight World Series victories over Los Angeles, Steinbrenner was still not content to rest languidly on his oars. He felt the pitching staff needed reinforcement if his club was to win a fourth consecutive

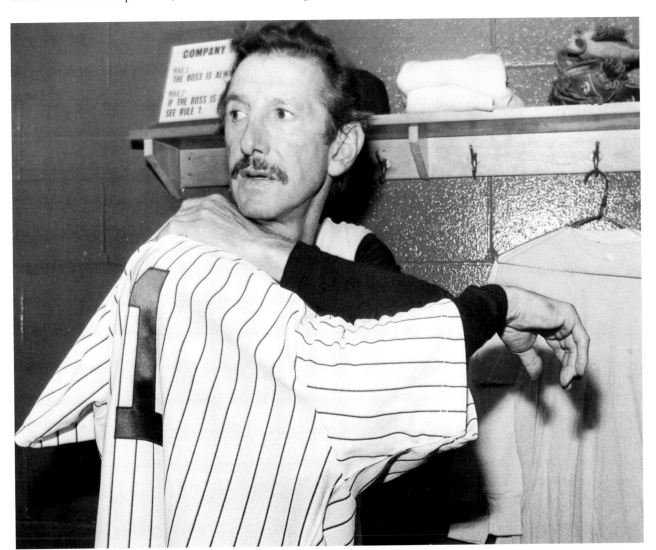

ABOVE: A LOOK OF APPREHENSION WAS UNDERSTANDABLE AS BILLY MARTIN DONNED HIS YANKEE UNIFORM SHORTLY AFTER OWNER GEORGE STEINBRENNER NAMED HIM TO MANAGE THE TEAM IN 1983. IT WAS MARTIN'S THIRD TOUR OF DUTY UNDER STEINBRENNER, BUT NOT HIS LAST. HE WAS FIRED AT THE END OF THE 1983 SEASON, HIRED AND FIRED IN 1985, AND HIRED AND FIRED AGAIN IN 1988.

OPPOSITE: DON MATTINGLY, HOMERING AGAINST THE OAKLAND A'S ON MAY 5, 1993. NO YANKEE FIRST-BASEMAN SINCE LOU GEHRIG EARNED AS MUCH ADMIRATION AS MATTINGLY DID DURING HIS YANKEE TENURE. ABOVE: WADE BOGGS, STROKING A BASE HIT IN THE YANKEES' HOME OPENER ON APRIL 4, 1994. IT WAS THE FIRST OF FOUR HITS HE REGISTERED AS THE YANKS BEAT THE TEXAS RANGERS 5–3.

pennant in 1979. So he plucked Tommy John, a south-paw who had survived a difficult elbow operation, from the Dodgers and also added Red Sox veteran Luis Tiant.

But an evil spirit seemed to hover over the Yankees. Baseball fights have invariably produced little more than tabloid headlines. But when the Yankees' big, mustached reliever, Goose Gossage, engaged in some horseplay with an equally large teammate, Cliff Johnson, the result was a bad sprain to Goose's right thumb. Half of the season went by before Gossage returned. With the other relief star, Sparky

Lyle, now on the Texas Rangers, the Yankees' bull pen was in need of help—and didn't get it.

The team floundered in fourth place. Thinking he could rejuvenate his troops, Steinbrenner fired Lemon in late June and replaced him with—you guessed it—Billy Martin. The Martin elixir, however, failed to work any wonders. Compounding the club's difficulties was the tragic death of Thurman Munson, the undisputed driving force of the team, an MVP in 1976 and a solid .300 hitter. Munson, an aviation buff, had purchased a twin-engine Cessna Cita-

> **You can talk until you're blue in the face about what it's like here and it doesn't matter until you experience it. The electricity that goes through here is unlike any other stadium. When Yankee Stadium is packed, the place is bigger than life.**
>
> **Willie Randolph,**
> **former Yankee player and**
> **current coach**

tion jet and loved to practice flying anytime the team had a day off. As the plane came in for a landing at the Akron–Canton, Ohio, airport on August 2, it crashed short of the runway and caught fire. Although the two other occupants of the plane survived, Munson didn't.

Already going through the motions, the Yankees were stunned by their teammate's death at the age of thirty-two. In the clubhouse the next day, Steinbrenner, his eyes flooded with tears, addressed the players, and Reggie delivered an inspirational speech about the lessons to be learned from tragedy, quoting from the Bible. The game that followed was a mournful and dreary exercise. The Yankees were sleepwalkers in uniform and lost, 1–0, to Baltimore, at the Stadium. The crowd came to say goodbye to the tough-as-nails Munson—and to a wrecked season. Curiously, when the campaign came to a close, the beleaguered Yankees announced they had drawn over 2½ million in attendance, a new record.

The scriptwriter for the season added one more dismal chapter. In October, Martin got into a squabble in a Bloomington, Minnesota, hotel bar, a not-uncommon venue for his misadventures. A marshmallow salesman ended up on the floor with a cut lip—and Billy ended up three days later with a dismissal from the enraged Steinbrenner, his third departure from a team that he claimed meant more than life to him.

Martin's successor was Dick Howser, a former infielder, college coach, and third-base coach under

Martin. Howser's admirers stressed that he was a quiet, unassuming guy. There was little that was tranquil about his season as pilot, however. The new president of the United States, Ronald Reagan, proclaimed it was "morning in America," but as far as Howser was concerned, it had become darkness at noon. Despite guiding the Yankees to a fine season (103 victories and a spot in the playoff against Kansas City), and with Reggie having his best year, Howser found he was still on the spot with Steinbrenner.

When KC demolished the Yankees in three straight games, thanks mainly to the slugging of George Brett, Steinbrenner leaked the news that he wasn't pleased with Howser. The owner's tactics forced Howser into a corner. It was clear that Dick had been fired, even if Steinbrenner preferred to consider it a resignation. Gene Michael, a former Yankees shortstop and recently named as the general manager, became New York's manager, as the team looked toward the 1981 season.

For some time, Steinbrenner had been casting longing eyes at an outfielder playing in San Diego. Dave Winfield, a college-bred, all-round athlete, with a reputation as a solid citizen, had become the biggest fish in the free-agent pool. Steinbrenner set out to sign him—and did. But it was costly. After the contract with Winfield was put through the computers, it amounted to about $20 million, spread over ten years.

But even more costly to both the Yankees and baseball was the strike called by the Players Association on June 12, at a moment when interest in the game was at an all-time high, with attendances and TV ratings zooming. Baseball had long been an American institution with poor guidance at the top and an almost nonexistent marketing approach. Those faceless people in charge took the game and its undisputed beauty, charm, skills, nuances, and wonderfully durable history for granted, much as Yankee dominance had been taken for granted. They assumed nothing could harm such an attractive commodity, not even their own malfeasance.

OPENING DAY OF THE 1996 SEASON FEATURED A SNOWSTROM AND A YANKEE VICTORY OVER THE KANSAS CITY ROYALS. MAN-
AGER JOE TORRE IS SEEN HERE RETURNING TO THE DUGOUT AFTER SOME WINTRY PREGAME CEREMONIES.

OPPOSITE TOP LEFT: SHORTLY AFTER THE IRT SUBWAY ROSE ABOVE GROUND, THIS GLIMPSE OF YANKEE STADIUM WAS PROVIDED. GENERATIONS OF SUBWAY RIDERS HAVE PRESSED THEIR FACES AGAINST THE TRAIN'S WINDOWS IN ANTICIPATION OF THIS TANTALIZING PREVIEW. OPPOSITE TOP RIGHT: ALONG RIVER AVENUE, ACROSS FROM YANKEE STADIUM, A LINE OF SOUVENIR SHOPS AND FAST-FOOD RESTAURANTS HAS BEEN PRESENT FOR DECADES. OPPOSITE MIDDLE LEFT: AS THEY HAVE FOR DECADES, VENDORS OUTSIDE THE STADIUM OFFER A TEMPTING ARRAY OF SOUVENIRS. OPPOSITE MIDDLE RIGHT: A WIDE-ANGLE VIEW OF YANKEE STADIUM, TAKEN IN JUNE 1996. ATTENDANCE WOULD IMPROVE AS THE YANKEES FLEXED THEIR PENNANT MUSCLES. OPPOSITE BOTTOM LEFT: CARE OF THE STADIUM PLAYING FIELD INCLUDES ATTENTION TO REAL GRASS. IN THIS PICTURE GROUNDSKEEPERS DANIEL CUNNINGHAM, ROBERT LAY, AND THOMAS FYFE APPLY NEW SOD. OPPOSITE BOTTOM RIGHT: EDDIE LAYTON, THE EXUBERANT YANKEE ORGANIST, HAS BEEN ENTERTAINING STADIUM CROWDS SINCE 1968. HE IS SEEN HERE DURING THE 1996 WORLD SERIES, PLAYING TO A PACKED HOUSE. ABOVE: THE MONUMENTS THAT STOOD IN DEEP CENTER FIELD BEFORE THE RENOVATION: LOU GEHRIG, MILLER HUGGINS, AND BABE RUTH.

After the strike was finally settled by August 10, play was resumed. But now something had to be done with a fractured season, so one of the game's hidden Euclideans came up with a "split-season" solution. The standings on June 12 were frozen, becoming the first half of the season. Division leaders at that stage were named first-half winners. Second-half winners would meet the first-half leaders in a three-out-of-five miniplayoff, to be concluded with the regular playoff between division champs. Most baseball aficionados regarded this plan with derision, for teams with the best overall record didn't get into postseason skirmishes. Having finished the first half on top, the Yan-

kees won the right to play in the first round of the playoffs, even though their cumulative record wouldn't have qualified them for postseason games. Oddly, though the Yankees were headed into postseason competition, Steinbrenner was already unhappy with Michael. Such unhappiness always meant a change of the guard. Michael was jettisoned the first week in September. Lemon's phone rang, and Steinbrenner rehired the man.

Lemon's usual equanimity helped the Yankees get through the remainder of the season. In the miniplayoff, his club beat Milwaukee, three games to two. Then they confronted their old recidivist pal, Billy

A few weeks after Mickey's death in August 1995, I visited Yankee Stadium with Mickey's boys, Mickey, Jr., David, and Danny, as part of a promotion for the Mickey Mantle Foundation. I had never sat in the stadium dugout before. When I looked over at the boys, I saw tears streaming down their faces. I was crying, too. It made me realize how much the stadium had truly been the center of their dad's life.

**Bill Liederman,
proprietor of Mickey
Mantle's Restaurant**

Martin, now managing Oakland. In a surprising overmatch against Martin's sorely overworked pitching staff, the Yankees took the first two games at Yankee Stadium, then wrapped it up with another victory at Oakland. And now who should be facing the Yankees in their thirty-third World Series? None other than the Los Angeles Dodgers, led by their super-salesman manager Tommy Lasorda. It marked the eleventh time around for a Yankees-Dodgers Series, going back to the days when the Dodgers hailed from Brooklyn.

The Yankees got off to a resounding start by whipping the Dodgers in the first two games at the Stadium. But the Yanks then split apart at the seams. They lost the next three games at Dodger Stadium. In the sixth game, back at Yankee Stadium, on October 28 (the latest game date in Series history, up to that time), the Dodgers won again, as a chilled crowd of over 56,000 watched glumly. Contributing to the Dodgers' World Series triumph was Yankee relief pitcher George Frazier, who lost three games in the Series, thus tying Claude Williams, the infamous Black Soxer, who purposely dropped three games in the 1919 Reds–White Sox Series.

In addition, Winfield, the expensive slugger, failed to slug very much. He followed a 1-for-13 performance against Oakland with only one hit in 22 at-bats against Los Angeles. There had once been a more mellow time, when a Series slump such as Winfield's could have elicited the ecumenical prayers of a borough. Gil Hodges' 0-for-21 against the Yankees in the 1952 Series won that kind of reaction from Brooklynites. But Steinbrenner was not in the mood for prayers for his employee. Instead, he issued an "apology" to the people of New York for his team's performance in the Series. No doubt he had Winfield mainly in mind, although other Yanks, including Reggie, did not perform as brilliantly as their boss might have hoped. Jackson was furious with Steinbrenner's statement. "I don't have anything to apologize for," he snarled. Winfield remained silent. The next year, Reggie was gone, having signed a five-year contract with the California Angels.

Steinbrenner's treacly message to the fans of the Yankees received almost as much attention as Edward VIII's renunciation of the British crown before World War II. It also became something of a symbolic watershed moment in the history of the Yankees, for over the next fourteen years the club completely lost their World Series habit. From the distressing loss to the Dodgers in 1981 through 1995, the Yankees failed to put in an appearance in the World Series, a competition in which they once seemed to own squatter's rights.

To be sure, there were memorable and significant moments during that arid span, including the interminable comings and goings of Billy Martin; the emergence of Don Mattingly as the most capable Yankees first-baseman since Gehrig; a no-hitter by Dave Righetti at the Stadium on July 4, 1983; the stigmatizing of Winfield by Steinbrenner, who was anointed as "Mr. May," in an obvious contrapuntal reference to Reggie, everybody's "Mr. October." There were occasional surges into contention on the part of the Yankees, but in the end the team didn't win any gonfalons.

One of the more nonproductive events at the Stadium took place on July 24, 1983, in a game against Kansas City. With New York leading, 4–3, in the top of the ninth, Brett, a constant harpoon in the belly of the Yankees, hit a two-run, two-out home run, giving his team a one-run lead. The ever-vigilant Martin, however, trotted out to the umpire to inform him that Brett's bat had pine tar on the handle that crawled up beyond the legal limit of 18 inches. Sure enough, it did, ruled the umps, and Brett was declared out, with the home run nullified and the Yanks winning, 4–3.

Led by an enraged Brett, the entire KC bench stormed out of their dugout in protest. Only the wise intercession of some of his teammates prevented Brett from decapitating Umpire Tim McClelland. An official protest was made by KC to the league office, and several days later American League president Lee MacPhail overruled the umps, restoring Brett's tainted home run into the record books. He also ordered the contest—now known as the Pine Tar Game—to be resumed, with KC ahead, 5–4. Figuring they had won a game because of the guile of their manager, the Yanks then protested MacPhail's decision. But MacPhail stood by his decree.

The game was finally completed when KC visited Yankee Stadium on an off day in August. After all the tumult, only 1,800 fans showed up to watch the anticlimactic proceedings. Three Yanks were retired summarily in the bottom of the ninth, and the Pine Tar Game became history.

Yogi Berra, always a popular figure in the Bronx, was back as Yankee manager in 1984, as the team finished third. Blossoming as an offensive threat, Mattingly won the American League batting crown after a sparkling duel with his teammate Winfield. The first Yankee to take such honors since Mantle had done it in 1956, Mattingly also demonstrated his skills as a defensive player. The next year, Mattingly added the Most Valuable Player Award to his achievements, all the

while remaining a counterbalance to the unsettled air that often permeated the Yankee clubhouse. But Don's efforts, plus the play of newcomer Rickey Henderson, the base-stealing genius, who had arrived from Oakland, still failed to head off Toronto, or preserve Yogi's job. Berra was gone in short order and Martin was back. In 1986, Mattingly again pounded out enough base hits and doubles, his specialty, to keep Yankee fans excited. But the batting title this time went to Boston's Wade Boggs, after a tight contest between the two players. It turned out to be only another second-place finish for the Yanks, as the Red Sox won the pennant.

From 1987 through 1991, the Yankees fell on hard times, and the Stadium became a place more of memory than accomplishment. (In 1988, however, the Yanks drew 2,633,701 to their home games, still an all-time mark for them.) But with the advent of William Nathaniel "Bucky" Showalter III, in 1992, things began to percolate again at the Stadium. Bucky was a diligent product of the Yankees' minor-league system. Nobody ever faulted Showalter's work ethic, for he was a managerial doppelgänger of Cal Ripken. He went to bed dreaming of lineup switches, scouted umpires to give his players a greater awareness of how balls and strikes would be called, and studied enemy pitchers with the persistence of Sherlock Holmes. Bucky's efforts paid off mightily for his team. Under his regime Jim Abbott, the former University of Michigan star who had been an Olympics hero, pitched the first no-hitter at the Stadium since Righetti's in '83. It came on September 4, 1993, against the power-laden Cleveland Indians and was doubly remarkable because of Jim's disability: he hurled without a right hand. When Abbott left the mound in the ninth inning, after retiring Carlos Baerga on a ground ball for the third out, the crowd of 27,225 erupted. It was a sweet moment for Abbott, Bucky, and the whole Yankee organization.

Showalter's overall winning percentage with the Yanks, from 1992 through 1995, was .539. In 1994, he was

RIGHT: YANKEE STADIUM DURING THE
HEAT OF THE 1996 CHAMPIONSHIP SEASON.
THE 120-FOOT-HIGH BOILER STACK REPLI-
CATES BABE RUTH'S BAT. THE FLAGS ARE
AT HALF STAFF IN HONOR OF MEL ALLEN,
WHO HAD PASSED AWAY JUST A FEW DAYS
EARLIER. BELOW LEFT: "PETE" SHEEHY
WAS IN CHARGE OF THE CLUBHOUSE FOR
NEARLY SIXTY YEARS. A PLAQUE CELE-
BRATING HIS TENURE IS AFFIXED TO THE
WALL OF THE YANKEE DUGOUT. BELOW
RIGHT: JACOB RUPPERT'S OWNERSHIP
LAUNCHED A DYNASTY. HIS PLAQUE COM-
MEMORATES HIS ROLE IN THE CONSTRUC-
TION OF YANKEE STADIUM.
OPPOSITE PAGE TOP LEFT: BATTING
PRACTICE AT THE STADIUM, WITH THE
USUAL GROUP OF REPORTERS, PHOTOGRA-
PHERS, AND VISITING PLAYERS IN ATTEN-
DANCE. OPPOSITE PAGE TOP RIGHT: THE
CLUBHOUSE, WHERE THE PINSTRIPES HANG
NEATLY. OPPOSITE PAGE MIDDLE LEFT:
A TIMELESS PREGAME RITUAL INVOLVES
SIGNING BASEBALLS, AND PART OF THE
RITUAL INCLUDES THE PLAYERS' COM-
PLAINTS AT HAVING TO ATTEND TO THE
TASK. OPPOSITE PAGE MIDDLE RIGHT:
THE MANAGER'S OFFICE IS SHORT ON LUX-
URY. JOE TORRE WAS THE OCCUPANT WHEN
THIS PICTURE WAS TAKEN DURING THE
1996 SEASON. OPPOSITE PAGE BOTTOM
LEFT: THURMAN MUNSON, THE YANKEE
CATCHER AND CAPTAIN, WAS KILLED IN A
PRIVATE PLANE ACCIDENT IN AUGUST
1979. SINCE THEN HIS LOCKER HAS BEEN
PRESERVED WITH HIS UNIFORM AND
CATCHER'S GEAR, IDENTIFIED ONLY BY HIS
UNIFORM NUMBER. OPPOSITE PAGE BOT-
TOM MIDDLE: THE PLAQUE DEDICATED TO
THE CAPTAIN'S LEADERSHIP. OPPOSITE
PAGE BOTTOM RIGHT: WADE BOGGS'S
LOCKER DURING THE 1996 SEASON. HIS
MAIL IS PILED UP ON HIS CHAIR, SEVERAL
PAIRS OF SHOES ARE NEATLY ARRANGED,
AND SOME GOOD-LUCK CHARMS CAN BE
SEEN ON AN UPPER SHELF.

THURMAN MUNSON
NEW YORK YANKEES
JUNE 7, 1947 - AUGUST 2, 1979
YANKEE CAPTAIN

"OUR CAPTAIN AND LEADER HAS NOT
LEFT US-
TODAY, TOMORROW, THIS YEAR, NEXT...
OUR ENDEAVORS WILL REFLECT OUR
LOVE AND ADMIRATION FOR HIM."

ERECTED BY
THE NEW YORK YANKEES

named Manager of the Year. All of these good deeds, plus the high regard in which he was held by the fans, appeared to assure Showalter's continued role after 1995. The wild-card Yankees had fought their way into the American League playoffs against Seattle in '95, serving further to underline Bucky's reputation as a skilled manager. It was his misfortune, however, to shepherd his flock through two victorious games at the Stadium, as the old edifice reverberated to the roars of over 57,000 in each game, only to watch the Mariners storm back to overcome the Yankees in the last three games at the Seattle Kingdome.

From start to finish, these games were gripping and tense, and the athletes performed with a July Fourth brio. Enjoying postseason play for the first time in fourteen years, the hungry Yankees faced a group of players every bit as hungry and talented as themselves. The confrontation injected juice into the bloodstream of the Yankees and into a game that many had rebuffed. It had been years since New Yorkers were able to immerse themselves into "Yankee baseball," and it produced a citywide euphoria. In addition, the fans could now applaud Mattingly, their veteran captain, who at last reaped the chance to play in the postseason. He put together five sparkling games, concluding the

series with a .417 average and six runs batted in, second only to outfielder Bernie Williams' .429.

At the end of the five cliff-hangers (ex-manager Wes Westrum of the Mets used to call such contests "cliff dwellers"), all of Mattingly's efforts were to no avail. The second game at the Stadium went fifteen innings and over five hours before Jim Leyritz of the Yanks hit a two-run homer. Limp from emotion, Yankee supporters were convinced that this would provide their team with the momentum to take one more game. But it didn't work out that way.

The New York–Seattle imbroglio was a healthy showcase for baseball, exhibiting the game to its full advantage. At the end, it was a burst of speed from the young legs of Seattle's Ken Griffey, Jr., that scored the run in the fifth game that carried the Mariners to victory.

Despite the disappointing loss, Steinbrenner said that he wanted to retain Showalter as manager. But then he asked Bucky to fire some of his coaches. The loyal Bucky didn't find this proposal easy to accept— and he refused. After almost two decades in the Yankees organization, Showalter decided to leave. In private, he cried. But not soon after he signed to manage the expansion club in Arizona.

I'll have great memories of this place. Obviously, it hurts losing, but the atmosphere here is matched nowhere. It's exciting to be out there on that mound in front of people going freaky. It's wild. Even though we lost, in a while we're going to appreciate being in this place.

> Greg Maddux,
> the Atlanta Braves pitcher,
> commenting after losing
> the sixth game of the 1996
> World Series

But what Showalter and the Yankees accomplished in 1995 boded well for the team's future. In the fall of '95 Bob Watson, a former Yankees player, was hired as the team's general manager, and he quickly selected Joe Torre, a nine-time All-Star and former manager of the Braves, Mets, and Cardinals, as the successor to Showalter. Watson explained that Torre was respected as a man, a leader, and a communicator. "He plays a brand of aggressive and exciting baseball," Watson said of Torre, who was the National League batting champion in 1971.

As the 1996 season unfolded, Watson proved to be prescient. The Yankees soon became the team to beat in the American League. Torre, a fifty-six-year-old, Brooklyn-bred man with a tough exterior, turned out to be a manager of equable disposition. Meanwhile, the restless Steinbrenner made some strategic moves that drew supportive cheers even from a normally hostile press. The owner insisted on signing Dwight Gooden, the one-time pitching wunderkind of the Mets, who was regarded as a lost cause by many because of his history of drug abuse. Confounding the baseball world, Gooden hurled a no-hitter at the Stadium on May 14 against Seattle, as 31,025 urged him on. In all his salad years with the Mets, Gooden, a consummate strikeout artist, had never pitched a no-hitter. In only his seventh start with the Yankees, Gooden was more emotional at the end of this game than he had ever

been in his life. He leaped in the air, pumped his fists, then talked about his father, Dan, waiting to undergo open-heart surgery in a Tampa, Florida, hospital.

"With all that I've been through and all that stuff that has gone on, this is the greatest feeling," Gooden said, his eyes bulging and his face glistening with beads of sweat.

It was a magical moment at the Stadium in a year that turned into a municipal soap opera. When George Steinbrenner also plucked another former Met, Darryl

OPPOSITE PAGE: THE STADIUM PRESS BOX OVERFLOWED WITH REPORTERS DURING THE 1996 WORLD SERIES. BELOW: IN THE FIRST GAME OF THE 1996 PLAYOFF SERIES AGAINST THE ORIOLES, DEREK JETER LOFTED A FLY BALL TO THE RIGHTFIELD WALL THAT WAS DEFLECTED BY A YOUNG FAN NAMED JEFF MAIER, WHO LEANED OUT AND DENIED BALTIMORE OUTFIELDER TONY TARASCO A CHANCE TO MAKE THE CATCH. IT WAS RULED A HOME RUN, DESPITE A LONG AND LOUD PROTEST BY THE ORIOLES. FOLLOWING PAGES: THE LAST OUT OF THE 1996 WORLD SERIES IS ABOUT TO BE RECORDED IN THIS PANORAMA PAINTED BY ANDY JURINKO. THIRD-BASEMAN CHARLIE HAYES IS RUNNING TOWARD THE THIRD-BASE GRANDSTAND IN PURSUIT OF MARK LEMKE'S POP-UP.

Strawberry, from the minor-league ash heap, his belief in another former drug abuser proved to be well founded. Strawberry acted with more maturity than he had before. As a part-time player, he contributed handsomely. On July 28 at the Stadium, he hit a game-winning home run, then followed that up on August 6 with a tour de force of three home runs—coming in quick succession in the second, fourth, and fifth innings—against the White Sox. The crowd of 33,025 seemed positively stunned at his comeback performance.

"I'm not finished yet," said Strawberry, who appeared composed and happy after years of turbulence and misery in his private life. Gooden and Darryl had been given second chances by Steinbrenner, and it had paid off.

On Sunday, August 25, with the sun high in the sky and the Yankees well on their way to a first pennant in fifteen years, over 50,000 fans journeyed to the Stadium to remember Mickey Mantle, dead for little more than a year. Only three Yankees icons—Miller Huggins, the Babe, and Gehrig—had previously been memorialized in the Stadium's Monument Park in center field, and now they unveiled the Mantle monument. The comedian Billy Crystal, who had worshiped Mantle when he was a kid—"I gave my Bar Mitzvah speech in an Oklahoma drawl and limped for no reason," he recalled—represented the millions of Mickey admirers in an emotional ceremony.

"Toward the end of Mickey's life," Crystal said, "a new person emerged. It was perhaps his finest hour."

There was simply no writing finish to the long-running melodrama of the 1996 season. After four months on the sidelines, David Cone, recuperating from surgery to remove an aneurysm and to have a vein grafted in his right shoulder, returned to active

OPPOSITE: GOT IT! CHARLIE HAYES AND THE FANS SAVOR THE EXACT MOMENT IN WHICH THE YANKEES HAVE CAPTURED THE WORLD CHAMPIONSHIP—THEIR TWENTY-THIRD, AND FIRST SINCE 1978, WHEN THEY ALSO SWEPT FOUR GAMES AFTER LOSING THE FIRST TWO.

My father took me to Yankee Stadium in the late forties, when I was about five years old. We lived in Brooklyn, a mile from Ebbets Field, but that first look at the stadium, with its green grass under blazing sunlight, was very exciting for me. I've been a Yankee fan ever since. The Yankees were playing the Red Sox that day, with Joe DiMaggio in center field for the Yankees and his brother, Dom, in center field for the Red Sox. But it seemed very strange to me that brothers would be playing on opposite teams, in the same position. I've been going to eight or ten games at the stadium every year, and now it's with my son, Andrew, who is as big a Yankee fan as I am.
Rudolph Giuliani,
mayor of New York City

duty on September 2 by pitching seven no-hit innings against Oakland. The game took place in Oakland, where Torre wisely removed Cone from the mound after 85 pitches. Cone proved that it takes a good deal more than fine-honed skill to make a superb pitcher. His competitive heart and desire, even as he remained cool as the underside of a pillow, was as important as his talent.

By September, the Yankees' long lead, which at one time was 12 games, over a Baltimore team that was hitting home runs by the carload, suddenly was whittled down to $2^1/2$ games. Again, Yankee tradition was at stake. In the process of winning thirty-three American League flags, the biggest first-place margin that the Yanks had ever wasted was a June 7 six-game lead in 1933. Eventually, that year, they finished six games behind the Washington Senators of Joe Cronin. In 1935, they mounted a $5^1/2$ game lead by June 20 but finished three games behind the Tigers. In 1987, the Yanks had a five-game edge on July 5 but it melted away in a fourth-place finish.

With games dwindling down to a precious few, Yankee fans began to sniff disaster as they visited the Stadium in the home stretch of the pennant race. Some were fearful that the Yanks would become the eighth team in history to blow a lead of 12 games. But as they had all year, the Yankees soon righted themselves, often coming from behind to win close games. On September 25, at the Stadium, they finally captured their thirty-fourth pennant by routing Milwaukee, 19–2.

All of this was accomplished with a team effort, headed up by a well-balanced roster. This was not a club of Babes, Lous, or DiMags. Rather, it was a team of largely unheralded players who took turns delivering the goods. For several years, Bernie Williams, a soft-spoken, shy, twenty-eight-year-old classical guitarist, from the tiny Puerto Rican town of Vega Alta, had been threatening to break through as a challenger to other wondrous Yankee center-fielders, men like DiMaggio, Earle Combs, and Mantle. At last seizing the imagination of the fans, Williams was covering the great swath of the Stadium's center field with a velvety smoothness that brought reassurance to Yankee followers. His bat also produced more clutch hits than it ever had before. Another Puerto Rican star, the late Roberto Clemente of Pittsburgh, had more charisma. But Williams' talent was now undeniable. At shortstop, another Yankee torn out of a storybook—Derek Jeter—played that position like a ten-year veteran. At twenty-two, Jeter knew the strike zone better than more experienced players. In the scorching cauldron of a pennant race, he consistently rose to the occasion, at bat and in the field. First-baseman Tino Martinez, acquired in the off-season, hit well enough to make Yankee fans grudgingly forget Don Mattingly, one of their all-time favorites. "Big Daddy" Cecil Fielder, the wide-bottomed home run slugger, came from Detroit in late season, pumping enough solid hits to show why Bob Watson had pried him loose from the Tigers.

In his second year, Andy Pettitte pitched with the cunning of Yankee southpaws of old, Lefty Gomez and Herb Pennock. Soon they would be comparing him with the all-time New York left-hander, the great Whitey Ford. Mariano Rivera, from Panama, and John Wetteland, with his sweat-stained cap, positively dominated the late innings of games with their determination and durability, as catcher Joe Girardi handled them with intelligence. When Girardi didn't catch, Jim Leyritz filled in with competence.

Others, like Paul O'Neill, bothered by injuries, and Tim Raines, once a slashing National League base stealer, came through when others didn't.

In short, this Yankee club was a resourceful, seemingly egoless group of marked ethnic diversity. The former New York mayor David Dinkins would have exclaimed that they were a gorgeous mosaic of blacks, whites, Latinos—and even one longitudinal Australian pitcher. They were kids, veterans, and reclamation projects, all handled with sureness and understanding by Torre, who in over thirty years in baseball had never gotten to the World Series.

In the two-tiered playoff system, the Yanks first went on to beat Texas by three games to one, although they trailed in each game and were bombarded for five home runs by Juan Gonzalez. The next confrontation was with Baltimore, conquerors of Cleveland. This battle with the Orioles would be the last hurdle before the World Series.

In the first game with the Orioles, on October 9, at Yankee Stadium, the Yankees were greeted by a sellout crowd, many of whom had queued up for hours to buy the tickets that were available. In a rare afternoon postseason game, what happened in the full light of day proved to be even more novel. With the help of a twelve-year-old New Jersey lad named Jeffrey Maier, who had come to the ball park armed with braces on his teeth and a black Mizuno fielder's glove, the Yanks miraculously pulled out a victory, after they had trailed, 4–3. In the eighth inning, Jeff became an instant hero to Yankee fans and a bête noir to Baltimoreans when he stuck out his glove in right field, preventing Tony Tarasco from making a play on Jeter's fly ball. Umpire Richie Garcia signaled home run on the drive, much to the consternation of Orioles manager Davey Johnson (and of many television viewers). That left it up to Williams to crush Baltimore with a game-winning home run in the eleventh inning.

The first instinct of the New York press was to canonize Jeff Maier. But soon he was chastised for his "illegal" pursuit of the vagrant fly ball. Jeff simply had done what any youngster would have done under the circumstances, however: he had reached out for a whizzing, seductive baseball hit by one of his heroes.

Although the Yanks lost, 5–3, in the next game at the Stadium, they surprised Baltimore by winning the next three games at Camden Yards, with Strawberry and Fielder playing important roles. For the first time since 1981, the team was in the World Series—and they could thank Jeff Maier and their own resiliency for their good fortune.

In the World Series against the Atlanta Braves, a team with the most vaunted pitching rotation since Koufax and Drysdale of the Dodgers, and with as close to a dynasty as baseball boasts in the 1990s, the Yankees distressed their supporters by losing the first two games at Yankee Stadium. Playing at home, the Yankees confronted cold and dreary weather, after New York had been exposed to a disastrous nor'easter. Then, in an amazing turnabout, the Yankees stormed into Atlanta's Fulton County Stadium, where they seized three games in a row, including the second contest in which they trailed by six runs. In

that one, Jim Leyritz's well-timed three-run homer put them back into contention. One could sense that the proud, puffed-up Atlantans were deflating on the spot.

On Saturday, October 26, on a crisp Bronx night at Yankee Stadium, before another roaring capacity audience, the Yankees surprisingly scored three runs against former Cy Young Award pitcher Greg Maddux. Then they held on to their lead, as the crowd held on to its breath. In the ninth inning, as Wetteland (ultimately the Most Valuable Player of the Series) pitched with the tying and winning runs on base, with two out, Charlie Hayes, the third-baseman acquired late in the season from Philadelphia, plunged into the Atlanta dugout pursuing a foul popup off the bat of Mark Lemke. TV announcer Tim McCarver suggested that Hayes and the Yankees should have been awarded the third out because of possible interference by a Braves player. The umpire didn't call it that way for New York, however, as was the case with Jeff Maier's amateurish intrusion. Seconds later, another foul pop, nearly in the same place, wound up in Hayes' glove. It was exactly 10:56 P.M., marking the final out of the twenty-third World Series title in Yankees history.

In addition, the Yankees again proved that they have a propensity for four-game Series wipeouts. Their teams of 1927, 1928, 1932, 1938, 1939, and 1950 had gone the four-straight victory route. The only difference now was that they had dropped the

FREE AGENCY WILL NO DOUBT THIN THEIR RANKS, BUT THESE SEVEN PLAYERS FORMED THE NUCLEUS OF A CHAMPIONSHIP TEAM IN 1996: DAVID CONE (OPPOSITE TOP LEFT), DEREK JETER (OPPOSITE TOP RIGHT), TINO MARTINEZ (OPPOSITE BOTTOM LEFT), MARIANO RIVERA (OPPOSITE BOTTOM RIGHT), PAUL O'NEILL (ABOVE), BERNIE WILLIAMS (BELOW LEFT), ANDY PETTITTE (BELOW RIGHT).

There are ghosts here and a rich tradition. You can sense it all around you. It's not just an invention of the press. When I was a youngster I rooted for National League teams and I sat in the stadium grandstand to watch Don Larsen's perfect World Series game in 1956. By the end of the sixth inning, I was rooting for Don to do it, even though I wasn't a Yankee fan. When I became manager here, the first time I walked down the runway leading to the dugout from the clubhouse I thought of Ruth and Gehrig and DiMaggio and all the others taking the same path. In my office there's a picture of Gehrig behind my desk. I inherited it, but I wouldn't think of removing it. That's what the stadium is about.
                        Joe Torre,
                        manager of the Yankees,
                        1996-

first two games in their own park before winning the last four.

Some were tempted to call this goose-pimple Series triumph—the first for New York since the Yanks defeated Los Angeles in 1978—a matter of destiny. Others dubbed it luck, others said it was karma. And some thought that *Mission Impossible* was less contrived. But the delighted crowd in Yankee Stadium, emitting constant roars and yelps that seemed to make the Stadium tremble and throb, didn't care what concatenation of the physical, metaphysical, or psychological had produced the astounding result. They simply loved it. So did the Yankee players— and, as it turned out, so did the entire city of New York, even some of those who had spent a lifetime despising the Yanks and their owner. The athletes embarked on a victory lap around the Stadium, Wade Boggs, his fist in the air, jumped on a policeman's horse, and nobody among the cheering and singing fans wanted to leave the premises.

"It's like there was an angel up there orchestrating this whole thing," said David Cone, a pale-faced man never at a loss for words.

"It's strange, weird," added manager Torre. "Like it was all supposed to happen."

As a sudden folk hero, Torre, whose family might have been cast in a Woody Allen movie, was involved in yet another subtext to the Yankee ascendancy. In June, Rocco, Joe's brother and a former police officer, had died suddenly of a heart attack. An older brother, Frank, once a major-league player with the Milwaukee Braves in the 1957 and 1958 World Series (against the Yankees), had been waiting for a new heart for several months in Columbia-Presbyterian Hospital, the identical plot of land on which almost a hundred years before the Yankees had played as the Highlanders. On Friday, an off day before what turned out to be the final game of the Series, Frank received his new heart—from a *Bronx* resident—and the successful operation was performed by a doctor fittingly named Oz!

The next day, Frank actually watched his brother's team triumph over the Braves on television, as he proudly wore his Yankee cap. He scarcely looked like a man whose life had been ebbing away only hours before.

Perhaps no Yankees season had ever come to such an improbable ending. It was topped off on October 29, three days after the clincher, by a tumultuous "ticker-tape" parade down Broadway's Canyon of Heroes in lower Manhattan, as millions of adoring New Yorkers, under a sea of Yankee caps and tissue paper, thundered their appreciation for a ball club that had gripped their hearts. Sometimes the crowd was twenty and thirty deep, but in all of their crazy

OPPOSITE: ALMOST THREE-QUARTERS OF A CENTURY AFTER THE FIRST FLAG WAS RAISED ABOVE YANKEE STADIUM, ANOTHER FLAG-RAISING CEREMONY TOOK PLACE ON APRIL 11, 1997, THIS TIME TO CELEBRATE THE 1996 WORLD CHAMPIONSHIP. THE FLAG-RAISERS INCLUDED FORMER YANKEE DON MATTINGLY, ON THE LEFT, YANKEE MANAGER JOE TORRE, AND RUDOLPH GIULIANI, THE MAYOR OF NEW YORK.

MICKEY MANTLE
"A GREAT TEAMMATE"
1931-1995

536 HOME RUNS
WINNER OF TRIPLE CROWN   1956
MOST WORLD SERIES HOMERS   18
SELECTED TO ALL STAR GAME   20 TIMES
WON MVP AWARD   1956, 1957 + 1962
ELECTED TO HALL OF FAME   1974

A MAGNIFICENT YANKEE
WHO LEFT A LEGACY OF
UNEQUALED COURAGE

DEDICATED BY
THE NEW YORK YANKEES
AUGUST 25, 1996

glee they acted, for the most part, decorously. The big city had turned into a small town of happy neighbors. When Torre addressed them, on the steps of City Hall, where the parade wound up, he asked, "How did everyone get into my living room?"

"For one day New York was like Emerald City," wrote columnist Bob Herbert. He also made the case that the Yankees belonged in the Bronx, in the history-filled old palace that had so often staged incandescent moments.

Beginning their season in the snowflakes of April, the Yankees had ended it in a hailstorm of "New York coleslaw."

As the 1997 season got under way, Jim Kaat, one of the Yankee broadcasters, issued a caveat: "You honor the past, but *don't* lean on it." Manager Torre appreciated what Kaat was saying and, in his own

One can see the stadium a thousand or more times. But to revisit it on Opening Day is like April in Paris. April in the Bronx. The real thing. The big ball park.
**George Vecsey,
columnist,
The New York Times**

inimitable low-key way, he prepared his team for a stiff challenge from the Baltimore Orioles.

Tim McCarver once said that "you never know a ball club until you've summered with it." The summer of 1997 proved to be almost as adventurous and hectic for the Yankees as their championship 1996 season. To begin with, as the Yankees picked up their championship rings, talk still percolated around New York about the ultimate destination of Yankee Stadium. Would the Yankees remain in the great ball park after 2002? Would there be a West Side Story, with the New Yorkers playing in a Manhattan venue, at a cost of over a billion dollars? Would they commit the heresy of moving to New Jersey? A poll taken in 1997 by the Marist Institute of Public Opinion revealed that the fans over-

whelmingly wanted the Yankees to remain in their 75-year-old home.

These were matters to be resolved in the near future. But Torre's main concern was with a ball club that would undergo any number of hurdles and traumas, as it rolled up 96 victories in the regular season and then won the wild card for the right to play Cleveland in the American League divisional competition.

Torre managed through the $15.8 million experiment with the overhyped and overweight pitcher from Japan, Hideki Irabu. A ringer for Babe Ruth, Irabu drew 51,000 fans to the Stadium on the night of July 10. The Yankees survived Irabu's temperament and inconsistency, as they also survived the stouthearted David Cone's bout with tendonitis that cost him a month on the mound. They held up through injuries to outfielder Bernie Williams, out for 33 games, and to Tim Raines, out for more games than that. They put up with Cecil Fielder's diminished home run productivity and Wade Boggs' hurt feelings, occasional clubhouse nastiness when veterans weren't chosen to play, and a hostile exchange between the mercurial southpaw David Wells and his boss, Mr. Steinbrenner.

In three remarkable days in mid-June, remarkable because of the fevered citywide interest on the part of Mets and Yankees fans, Yankee Stadium became the raucous headquarters for a reinvigorated interborough rivalry. Not even a heated rent-control controversy in the city could deflect the hoopla about the two ball clubs. The Yankees and Mets had never played each other in regular season games, and now interleague play had given the upstart Mets an opportunity to upend the world champions.

The Mets did just that in the first game, before 56,000 fans, as Dave Mlicki threw the first shutout of his career. The next night the Yankees retaliated with a 6–3 victory before another sellout crowd. The third game, on the cloudy afternoon of June 18, was the most dramatic. It featured a "foul home run," a crucial game-tying balk, and six no-hit innings by Cone. The Yankees finally won

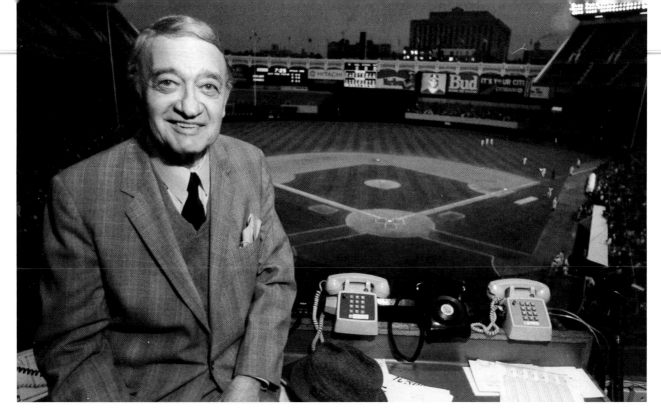

PREVIOUS PAGES: ON AUGUST 25, 1996, MICKEY MANTLE'S PLAQUE WAS ADDED TO MONUMENT PARK. A LOYAL FAN, WEARING A REPLICA OF MANTLE'S JERSEY, READS THE TRIBUTE. ABOVE: IN APRIL 1990, MEL ALLEN RETURNED TO THE YANKEE STADIUM BROADCASTING BOOTH AND WORKED AN INNING AND A HALF OF A GAME BETWEEN THE YANKEES AND THE OAKLAND ATHLETICS. HE SHOULD HAVE BEEN INVITED TO WORK LONGER. FORTUNATELY FOR THOSE WHO COULD APPRECIATE HIS TALENTS, MEL COULD BE HEARD WEEKLY ON THE HIGHLIGHTS SHOW "THIS WEEK IN BASEBALL."

the ten-inning struggle, 3–2. In three tumultuous days of fun and noise the Stadium rocked to the roar of over 170,000 people, the most for a three-game set since the Stadium underwent a facelift in 1976.

An unaccustomed moment of tenderness took place on the night of August 30. Before over 55,000 admiring fans former Yankee first-baseman Don Mattingly was honored and his number 23 was retired. "This was a great place to play for me," Mattingly said. "This city is a result-oriented city. I was able to play ball and get plenty of attention for that. I was able to be myself." Thus Mattingly, a thorough professional not given to effusiveness, joined other Yankees in having his number enshrined: Gehrig (4), 1939; Ruth (3), 1948; DiMaggio (5), 1952; Mantle (7), 1969; Stengel (37), 1970; Bill Dickey and Berra (8), 1972; Whitey Ford (16), 1974; Thurman Munson (15), 1979; Maris (9), 1984; Elston Howard (32), 1984; Rizzuto (10), 1985; Billy Martin (1), 1986; Reggie Jackson (44), 1993.

In the windup to the '97 season, the Yankees roared back from a 5–0 deficit in the first postseason game against Cleveland with record-setting back-to-back-to-back home runs by Tim Raines, Derek Jeter, and Paul O'Neill. However, in the second game at the Stadium the Indians defeated the Yankees before a jam-packed house.

When the series moved to Cleveland, Paul O'Neill, an intense, brilliant performer all year, hit a home run with the bases loaded to win the third game. It appeared that the Yankees were on their way to confront Baltimore in the next postseason round. However, a home run by Sandy Alomar in the eighth inning of the fourth game, when the Yankees were only four outs away from victory, threw the team into reverse. The following night the Yankees lost a squeaker to Cleveland's tight defense and a twenty-one-year fireballer named Jaret Wright, who reminded some people of Bob Feller.

There would be no more games at Yankee Stadium in 1997. October had turned cold for New York. Even George Steinbrenner was moved to say, "Wait 'til next year," echoing that ancient sad song of Brooklyn Dodgers fans.

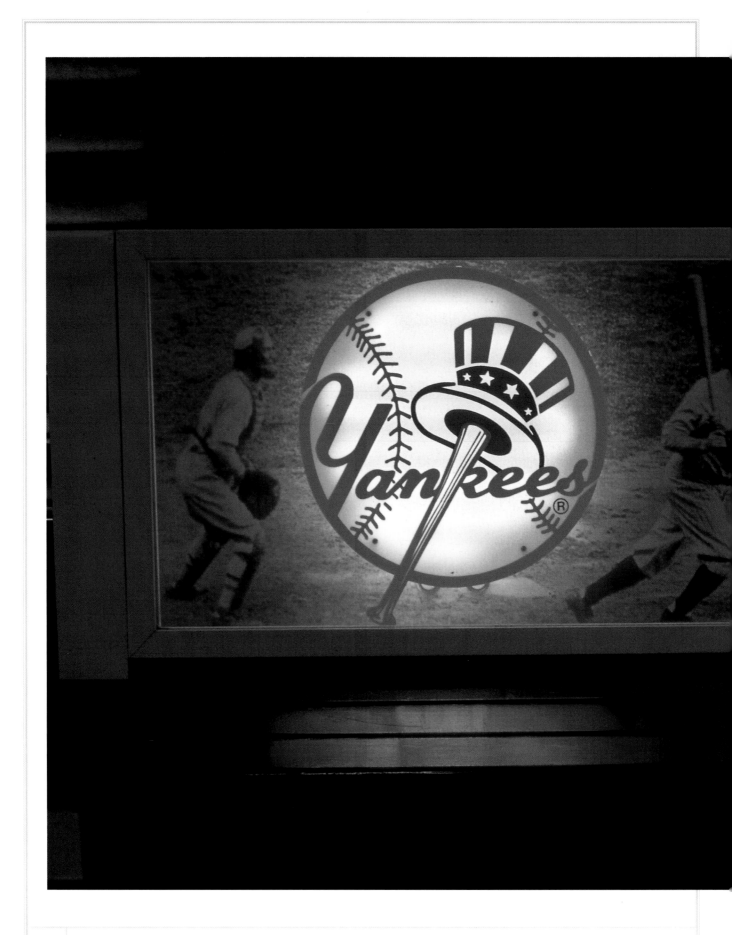

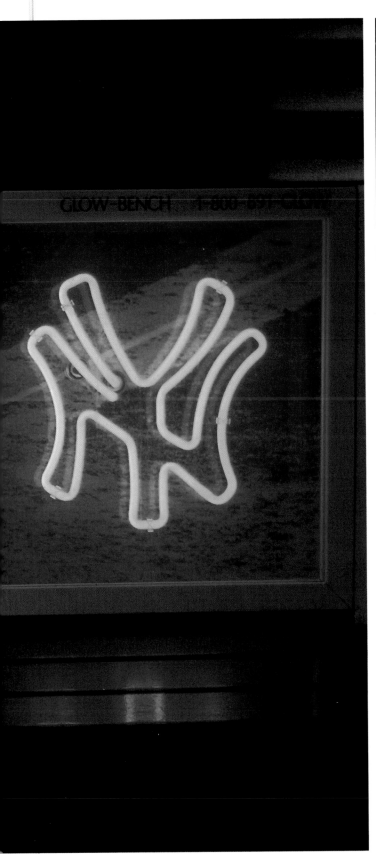

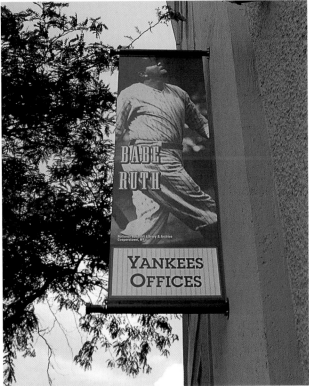

OPPOSITE: THROUGHOUT THE BALL PARK "GLOW BENCHES" ARE SPOTTED, ILLUMINATING THE LOGO AND A RUTHIAN HOME RUN. ABOVE TOP: YANKEE FANS CLAPPING, CHEERING, AND YELLING. AND NO DOUBT A FEW LEATHER-LUNGED FANS ARE LETTING A PLAYER KNOW EXACTLY WHAT THEY THINK OF HIM. ABOVE BOTTOM: ENTRANCES TO YANKEE STADIUM ARE EMBELLISHED WITH REMINDERS OF THE BALL PARK'S STORIED PERFORMERS. FOLLOWING PAGES: A GROUND-LEVEL VIEW OF MONUMENT PARK, AND SOME OF THE PLAQUES HONORING YANKEE HEROES.

Index

McDougald, Gil, *94,* 99, 101

McGeehan, W. O., 5, 21

McGraw, John J., 1, 3, 4, 5, 6, 9, 12, 26, 48

Mack, Connie, 7, 41, *90*

Mack, Gene, *90*

McKechnie, Bill, 50

MacNamee, Graham, 21

MacPhail, Lee, 151

MacPhail, Leland Stanford "Larry," 68–69, 70

retirement of, 71–75

McQuinn, George, 70

McWilliams, Tom "Shorty," 47

Maddux, Greg, 155, 163

Maglie, Sal, 99

Maier, Jeffrey, *155,* 163

Maloney, Jim, 36

Mantle, Mickey Charles, 81, 83, 86, 99, *104,* 110, 114, 116, *117,* 118, 119–22, *135,* 151, 171

almost-out-of-the-stadium home run of, 122, 123

injuries of, *94, 104,* 114, 115, 119–22

monument to, 159, *171*

Mapes, Cliff, *83*

Maranville, Rabbit, 51

Maris, Roger, 110, 114, 115, 116, 118, 119, 171

Ruth's record broken by, 114–15, *117, 122*

Martin, Billy, 86, 88–89, 100, 134, 139–42, *143,* 145, 146, 149–50, 151, 171

Jackson and, 138, 139, 141–42

Martinez, Tino, 162, *165*

Mathewson, Christy, 50

Mattingly, Don, *145,* 150, 151, 154, *166,* 171

Mauch, Gus, 78

Maxim, Joey, 88

Mays, Carl, 19, *41*

Mays, Willie, 81, 116

Mazeroski, Bill, 110

Mercer, Sid, 55

Merrill, Robert, 119

Meusel, Bob, 10, 24

Michael, Gene, 146, 149

Miller, Ray, 88

Milwaukee Braves, 100, 162, 166

Minnesota Twins, *135*

Mitchell, Dale, 99

Mize, Johnny, *94*

Mlicki, Dave, 170

Moore, Marianne, 119, *127*

Moore, Wilcey, *101*

Munson, Thurman, 122, *135,* 138, 139, 141, 171

death of, 145–46, *152*

Murcer, Bobby, 122–25

My Baseball Diary (Farrell), 56

Myhra, Steve, 109

National Football League, *see* NFL

National League, 40, 59

Nauen, Elinor, 118, 142

Navin, Frank, 6

Nettles, Graig, *141,* 143

Neun, Johnny, 69

New York Evening Telegram, 13

New York Giants, *viii,* 1, 3, 4, 5, 7, 8, 9, 12, 48, 52, 55, 89

in 1921 Series, 10

in 1923 Series, 21, 24–25, 26

in 1951 Series, 79, *94*

in 1962 Series, 116

westward move of, 100

New York Giants (football), 100–109, *110,* 116

New York Mets, 118, 126, 170–71

New York Times, 17, 21, 24, 36, 48, 72, 170

New York World, 25

New York Yankees:

CBS ownership of, 118, 126, *127*

farm system of, 59

as Highlanders, *viii,* 1, 2–5, 166

1953 Old-Timers Game of, *101*

numbered jerseys worn by, 41

origin of name, 4–5

sold by Ruppert heirs, 68

world titles of, 25

New York Yankees (football), 36

NFL (National Football League), 36, 100, 105, *110,* 116

Notre Dame, 32–35, 40, *41, 47, 88*

O'Farrell, Bob, 35

Old-Timers Game, *101*

O'Malley, Walter, *127*

O'Neill, Paul, 162, *165,* 171

Osborn Engineering Company, *19*

Paige, Satchel, 91

Parker, Dan, 57

Paschal, Ben, 36

Paul, Gabe, 126

Peckinpaugh, Roger, 4, 8, *101*

Pennock, Herb, 10, 19, 40, *41,* 53

Perlman, Itzhak, 116

Pettitte, Andy, 162, *165*

Philadelphia Athletics, *34,* 37, 41–44, *41,* 62

Pipgras, George, *41*

Pipp, Wally, 6–7, 8, 18, *101*

Pittsburgh Pirates, 40, 110

Players Association strike, 146–49

Podres, Johnny, 91–97

Polo Grounds, *viii,* 3, 4, 6, 8, 9, *10,* 12, 25, 32, *51,* 68, *90*

fire in, 4

Price, Jim, 4

Purdom, Bill, *10, 122*

Putnam, Ambrose, 3

Acknowledgments

. . . .

With special thanks to Richard J. Cerrone, Public Relations Director for the New York Yankees, for his splendid cooperation. And thanks also go to Gregg Mazzola and Leo Trachtenberg for research material that they provided.

—R. R.

Picture research was aided greatly through the kind efforts of Elvis Brathwaite and Bill Fitzgerald at AP/Worldwide, Laura Tosi at the Bronx County Historical Society, Carol Butler at Brown Brothers, Allan Reuben at Culver Pictures, Darci Harrington at The National Baseball Hall of Fame and Museum, Bill Martin at *The New York Daily News*, Jocelyn Clapp and Norman Currie at Corbis/Bettman, and Rick Cerrone from the New York Yankees. Original photographs in the book are the work of Pete Schroeder and Andy Jurinko, whose splendid paintings also grace these pages. Thanks to Bill Purdom for his paintings, and to Bill Goff for his assistance and patience. Thanks also to Renato Stanisic for the handsome design, and at Penguin Studio thanks go to our publisher, Michael Fragnito, and to Roni Axelrod, who handled production. Finally, the undertaking was guided skillfully by our editor, Christopher Sweet, whose enthusiasm made the entire effort a pleasure.

—C. J.

Illustration Credits

. . . .

AP/Wide World Photos: pp. 45, 53, 67, 72, 73, 78, 80, 87, 95, 104, 111, 115, 123, 124, 127, 131, 135, 136, 140, 143, 144, 145, 158, 167, 171; Archive Photos: pp. 90, 160; Reprinted Courtesy of *The Boston Globe:* p. 90; Brigandi Coin Co.: pp. 92, 98, 102; Courtesy of the Bronx County Historical Society, New York City: pp. 91, 106, 132; Brown Brothers, Sterling, Pa.: pp. 21, 32, 33, 38, 39, 54, 58, 105; Culver Pictures: pp. 32, 34, 44, 53, 84; Courtesy Dr. Lloyd Feinberg: p. 30; Courtesy M. Frank: pp. 20, 74, 96; Bill Goff, Inc.: pp. 10, 48, 108, 120, 156; © John Henderson, H&H Productions: p. 125; Christopher Jennison Collection: facing p. 1 (top and bottom), pp. 22, 23, 27, 51, 57, 61, 66, 79, 88, 101, 105, 117, 127, 130; Courtesy Andy Jurinko: pp. 148, 153; © David Lilienstein, David Lilienstein Photography: pp. 148, 154; National Baseball Hall of Fame and Library, Cooperstown, N.Y.: pp. 24, 25, 41, 83; *The New York Daily News:* pp. 16, 46, 147, 155, 168; Courtesy New York Yankees: p. 122; PF Sports Images: pp. 82, 164, 165; © 1996 DD & E. Peter Schroeder: title page, pp. 148, 149, 152, 153, 172, 173, 174; Courtesy Marc Simont: p. 122; Courtesy Richard J. Solomon: p. 125; UPI/Corbis-Bettmann: facing title page, pp. 14, 16, 17, 18, 28, 37, 42, 47, 50, 64, 66, 67, 76, 89, 94, 110, 112, 128.

Afterword

. . . .

Despite the disappointment of 1997, now it was time for the emergence of still another era of Yankees omnipotence. Few could have anticipated that the poised Torre would lead his team to one World Series victory after another, thereby joining his much-acclaimed predecessors Huggins, McCarthy, and Stengel. By winning pennants and World Series in 1998, 1999, and 2000, Torre not only established his credentials as a master tactician and diplomat, but also proved it was possible to survive the heated media environment of New York as well as the constant effluvia emanating from the Yankee front office.

In those three World Series triumphs Torre's men defeated the San Diego Padres, Atlanta Braves, and New York Mets. In the process they lost only a single game, to the Mets, the kind of total devastation that had been associated with the squad of Babe and Lou and the team of DiMaggio and Mantle.

Brian Cashman came on as general manager of the Yankees in 1998—the second youngest man ever in that role in the game's history—and he made some shrewd acquisitions, including veteran outfielder Chili Davis, third baseman Scott Brosius, who had just suffered a miserable year in Oakland, and second baseman Chuck Knoblauch, from Minnesota. But perhaps the most celebrated addition was the Cuban émigré pitcher, Orlando (El Duque) Hernandez, who won a four-year contract from the Yankees after escaping from his native Cuba.

Oddly, the magic year of 1998 began with three straight losses, but from that time on the team was close to unbeatable. At season end the Yankees had won 114 games, second only to the Chicago Cubs of 1906, who captured 116 games under manager Frank Chace. Those Yankee wins included the second perfect game in Yankee history, produced by David Wells, against Minnesota on May 17 at Yankee Stadium.

By the end of the 1998 season the Yankees were 66 games over .500 and 22 games ahead of the blighted Boston Red Sox, the widest margin in Yankee history. Batting at the bottom of the formidable Yankee lineup, Brosius was named MVP of the World Series, as the Yankees finished the year with seven straight postseason victories.

In spring training of 1999 the doctors told Joe Torre he had prostate cancer. He turned the reins of the club over to his dugout sidekick, Don Zimmer. In Joe's absence, Zimmer managed the club to a 29–20 mark. In June, Roger Clemens served notice that he still had the zip on his fast ball as he registered his eighteenth straight triumph. (By midseason of 2003, Clemens reached his sought-after target of over 300 career wins, at which he announced his intention of retiring from baseball after the year.)

Perhaps the biggest surprise of 1999 was David Cone's perfect game against Montreal in July. The right hander joined Yankees Don Larsen and Wells in the charmed contingent of pristine pitchers. In delivering his masterpiece, Cone threw only 20 called balls and struck out 10 batters. Several days after Cone's game the Yankees tallied 21 runs versus Cleveland, the most runs scored by them at Yankee Stadium since 1931.

The Yankees total of 98 wins in 1999 suffered by comparison to the '98 output, but it was enough to put them in the winner's circle again—their third flag in four years. Jeter continued to get better. This time he amassed 219 hits, with a .349 average, clearly convincing Yankee adherents that he merited consideration as the all-time Yankee shortstop.

In the postseason the Yankees were nearly invincible. They took three straight from Texas and three out of five from the Red Sox as they advanced to the World Series. As usual, Atlanta was on hand for the National League but the Yankees banged the Braves around in a four-straight wipeout, causing millions of New Yorkers to celebrate the Yankees' latest achievement—their twenty-fifth world crown. The town's ultimate Yankee fan, Mayor Rudy Giuliani, was on hand at City Hall to lead the cheers.

Defying all odds, the Yankees did it again in 2000. Searching for a third straight world title, to equal Oakland's feat from 1972 to 1974, the Yankees were populated with graybeards like the thirty-seven-year-old Paul O'Neill, thirty-three-year-old Tino Martinez, and the thirty-three-year-old Brosius. The performance of the team in the opening months possibly reflected this weariness. In addition, Cone started to lose more games than he won. At this stage, the Yankees pried David Justice loose from Cleveland, and he became a catalyst for the team. He hit 20 late-season home runs for New York, many of them key blows, which established him as the serendipitous player of the year.

From July 1 to mid-September the Yankees awoke from their slumber, going 44–22, to take charge of the American League race. With three weeks to go, the Yankees inexorably moved ahead of the usual suspects in Boston, reinforcing the notion that the Red Sox were truly snake-bit or constant victims of the Curse of the Bambino.

There was, however, a negative highlight of the season. That moment arrived when the Mets slugger Mike Piazza was hit in the helmet by an errant pitch (was it really errant?) thrown by Clemens during an interleague game. The pitcher has long had a reputation as a "head hunter" and the fact that early in the year Mike clubbed a bases-loaded homer off Clemens fueled the rampant suspicion that Clemens knew precisely what he was doing.

In the World Series who should wind up against the Yankees but the Mets, who would compete in the fourteenth Subway Series in New York history. The last time there had been an intracity competition was in 1956, when the Brooklyn Dodgers lost to the Yankees in seven games. The citizenry of the city became maniacally involved in the Mets–Yankees conflict, although the rest of the country took the whole affair in stride. Few outside of New York cared very much whether the Yankees could win again or if the Mets could pull off an underdog victory.

After a first game at packed Yankee Stadium that went 12 innings and almost five hours, the Yankees emerged with the win. They took the second game, too, but after a bizarre incident once again involving Clemens and Piazza. Clemens's pitch to Piazza in the first inning splintered Mike's bat. The barrel stayed in Piazza's hand while another cracked segment of the bat bounced out toward Clemens. The always-intense pitcher seized the wood, almost as if he were fielding it, and in the same motion he hurled it in the direction of Piazza, who was chugging towards first base. The ball, meanwhile, ended up in foul territory near first base. Luckily, the splintered portion of the bat missed Piazza, who later, for the life of him, couldn't quite figure out what Clemens had intended. However, many viewers, including those covering the game on TV, felt Clemens's action was indefensible.

After the tumult subsided, Clemens held the Mets at bay while the Yankee bats went to work. The win put the Yankees ahead, two games to none. In game three, El Duque, so tough in postseason contests, was on the mound for the Yankees, presumably sending his team on the way to another four-game sweep. This time Hernandez failed, but not by much. He fanned 12 Mets, the most that any Yankee hurler had chalked up in a World Series game. However, the Mets pushed across a go-ahead run in the eighth inning and El Duque, pitching despite the flu, took the loss.

That sent the series back to Shea Stadium, where Derek Jeter banged a home run on the first pitch of the fourth game. Mets fans were plunged into gloom. The Yankees took that fourth game and then the fifth, with an unlikely hero, Luis Sojo, the priceless utility man, connecting for the crucial hit of the final game. At exactly midnight Piazza smashed a ball to deep center field. If it had gone over the wall, the Mets would still have been alive, but the ball landed in Bernie Williams's glove—and the Yankees were victorious once again.

The Yankees had won their fourth title in five years and their third in a row. In the twenty-five years since the advent of free agency the Yankees were the only team to capture three straight World Series. Torre, once scoffed at as a manager, was 16–3 in Series competitions, better than any man who ever managed in more than one Series.

In the aftermath of a bitter presidential election between Al Gore and George W. Bush, followed by the ghastly and murderous events of September 11, the Yankees, as preoccupied as other millions were at the time, still won their league title. But as they pursued their fourth consecutive championship, they finally faltered. It took a dramatic seven games, but the Arizona Diamondbacks came out in front, after the thirty-fourth seventh game in Series history. It took two magnificent pitchers, Randy Johnson and Curt Schilling (who won all four games between them), to stop the Yankees.

The next year, the Yankees were dominant again in their division, but the low-budget Anaheim Angels stopped them. Whatever combination of factors propel the Yankees as they continue to dampen the hopes of other clubs, they remain baseball's greatest franchise, playing in the game's most hallowed amphitheater.